THE LOVE OF MONEY
How to Build Wealth and Not Be Corrupted

THE LOVE OF MONEY

How to Build Wealth and Not Be Corrupted

Rodney Ballance

AMBASSADOR INTERNATIONAL
GREENVILLE, SOUTH CAROLINA & BELFAST, NORTHERN IRELAND

THE LOVE OF MONEY

How to Build Wealth and Not Be Corrupted

ISBN: 978-1-935507-22-2

Cover Design & Page Layout by David Siglin of A&E Media

AMBASSADOR INTERNATIONAL
Emerald House
427 Wade Hampton Blvd.
Greenville, SC 29609, USA
www.ambassador-international.com

AMBASSADOR BOOKS
The Mount
2 Woodstock Link
Belfast, BT6 8DD, Northern Ireland, UK
www.ambassador-international.com

The colophon is a trademark of Ambassador

Dedication

Throughout this book, you will read about the importance of building a strong foundation to your financial portfolio.

As important, if not more so, is the importance of building a strong moral foundation in the lives of our children.

I'd like to dedicate this book to my parents, Ann and Rodney Ballance, Sr. for doing just that in my life. Even though I veered away from what I knew to be right at times, I was able to turn back and lead an honorable life because they raised me with a good strong foundation.

The Bible says "Train up a child in the way he should go, and when he is old he will not depart from it", Proverbs 22:6.

It is my desire that our children Jonathan, Sarah, and Nick will have the same strong foundation that will enable them to build productive lives for generations yet to come.

Thanks Mom and Dad for giving me a determination to succeed, and a clear understanding between right and wrong.

Table of Contents

Chapter One

Diagnosing the Situation

$

If you were happy with your financial situation, you wouldn't be looking for ways to improve it.

In this book, we're going to compare what you've heard and accepted as fact, against a fresh, different and encouraging way to view financial planning. Everyone's situation is different, and for that reason, I don't believe that you should ever follow a "one-size-fits-all" approach when it comes to your finances. I've said so to millions of people on national radio and television programs over the past couple of years.

100% of my clients made money during the recession of 2008. Did you?

For those of you who don't know, I am the host of a nationally syndicated radio program called "Ballancing Your Budget" available over numerous radio stations and through live streaming over the internet.

I've also been blessed to have been a regular contributor for the American Family Radio network. As I am writing this book I am also the financial expert, and regular contributor for CBN News (Christian Broadcasting Network) which is the home of The 700 Club.

People who want you to buy their books, however, may have a different spin on what they are trying to sell you, but most of these books tell you the same old thing: Pay off your house as soon as you can by sending the bank all of your money; pay only cash for everything; and always put what's left over in the stock market, because that's the only way you'll ever have enough money to put your kids through college or fulfill your retirement dreams.

The reason these books always give you the same tired advice is that they're easy to write and generate large amounts of money for those who write them. The only ones benefiting from a lot of this so-called financial advice is the person who wrote the book. You know what I'm talking about. How many books or programs have you looked at? How many of them tell you basically the same thing?

The kind of financial planning I'm talking about isn't just rubber stamping an idea and telling everyone to line up and follow it. But if you are the kind of person who likes having choices and making your own decisions based upon sound and reliable advice, you will absolutely love the financial planning approach I recommend for your financial future.

In 2009 I formed a not for profit ministry named The Abundant Life Institute (A.L.I.) as the method of distributing competent information to the people who were searching for it. The concept for A.L.I. came to me after reading about the great work done by other professionals through an organization called "Doctors without Borders". I was inspired by the selfless way those professionals volunteered their time and talents to help people in need of improving their physical well being.

Implementing that same volunteer philosophy, I believed that there were Christian financial professionals who would be willing to help people who were searching for help to improve their financial well being. Through our network of Christian financial professionals that we refer to as "Money Coaches", we successfully employ an investing approach known as "The Trinity Plan," because of its emphasis on three godly principles:

» **Enrich** people with knowledge
» **Encourage** people with confidence
» **Empower** them with continued Christian support

At the end of this book, I'll provide you with a sample report that our staff generates for everyone who asks us to help them design a financial plan for their family. The work is done for free through our ministry. We'll talk about specifics at length later in the book.

As one example of how damaging a "one-size-fits-all" philosophy can be, I'd like to tell you about a couple I met with recently who allowed greed to destroy their hopes of a comfortable retirement. I met with these nice folks, whom we'll call Mr. and Mrs. Jones, in August of 2008. Their daughter, a client of mine, had grown increasingly concerned over her parent's financial situation for some time. They had a portfolio worth more than $700,000, yet they were writing bad checks at the grocery store and depending on their daughter for financial assistance. What had happened?

I found the answer when I reviewed their portfolio. Mr. and Mrs. Jones, 65 and 62 years old, had worked for the same company for many years and earned several thousand shares of the company stock. The asset manager told them to hold onto all of their shares, and not to sell. Mr. Jones retired a year before our meeting, but retained his stock. Mrs. Jones was drawing disability, but wanting to retire when she had enough money to do so comfortably. They were depending on the asset manager of their company plan, and peers at work for their financial advice.

I was baffled about why they were writing bad checks when they had more than enough to comfortably retire. I showed them how they could take the money they had earned and use it to provide a lifetime income for themselves and also leave a nice legacy for their children and grandchildren.

I discovered the reason for their hesitation after realizing why their company stock had increased so dramatically from the $20 range, where it had been for the past 30 years, to its new high of over $250 per share: China had taken advantage of the strength of their currency and the extreme buying power they had because of the weakening of the U.S. dollar. China was stockpiling huge amounts of the company's product to use at a later date for a fraction of the normal cost.

"A fool and his money are soon parted."
—Thomas Tusser
16th century author

By the time I was ready to make a recommendation, though, the dollar had begun strengthening again, which consequently drove down the stock price. That solidified my belief that the reason for the soaring stock price was due to the once-in-a-lifetime anomaly caused by the exceptional demand for this company's product overseas. Once the demand and the attractive buying opportunity was gone, however, the stock price would return to a much lower level, and would most likely remain there for many years to come.

I used charts to support my theory and drive home the point that this had been a great ride, but now was the time for them to sell their holdings and get into a fixed-rate financial vehicle that would provide a substantial lifetime income for them. That's when I heard the words that haunted me for months:

"But we're so close to a million dollars," Mrs. Jones said. "We just need to hold on to it, and I know we will be millionaires. Everyone at work is telling us to hold on to our stock because our company is doing so well." Listening to co-workers about your finances can lead you to disaster, and unfortunately, that's exactly what happened to these nice folks.

Mr. and Mrs. Jones held on to their stock, and it continued its downward spiral as the U.S. dollar strengthened. When China stopped buying their product, the stock fell to about $60 per share – a $210 per share loss from what it had been when I made my recommendation five months earlier. Now they have a little over $100,000 left. That's still a nice lump sum, but not enough to sustain the comfortable retirement they could have enjoyed.

Sometimes making the money isn't the hardest part of building a successful portfolio; it's knowing where to get the advice that will allow you to keep it that counts. If the asset manager had been looking out for the company's employees, he would have seen the same things I did, and warned them about the impending danger. Instead he advised company employees to keep the stock so he could continue making money off of them. Word to the wise: Usually the person who signs you up for your supplemental retirement plan at work isn't the right person to ask about allocating your assets. It's only fair to note here that asset managers derive personal income through fees and recurring charges to your account.

Now let's look at a fresh approach to money; an approach that will not only make you more money, but will set you apart from others who simply line up to blindly follow the latest trend, such as investing in junk bonds or hedge funds.

Thomas Tusser, (1524-1580) was an English author, poet, musician, and farmer. He's best known for his instructional poem

"One Hundred Points of Good Husbandry." This famous statesman once said "A fool and his money are soon parted". That's especially true when people want something for nothing, or want to turn a little bit into a whole lot in a hurry, but fail to see or care about potential consequences.

Rarely does anyone step out on faith and try to tell people things that aren't in keeping with what the masses are hearing, but that's our mission at The Abundant Life Institute. I have taken my secular business and transformed it into a ministry where we help anyone who wants help at no cost. I ask that people attend one of our Financial Empowerment Workshops first to get an understanding of the basic ideas and concepts we use.

One thing is certain: Those who have access to, and control over, their money will always prevail during challenging economic times!

All of my clients made money during our nation's recent economic crisis. That's right, *every one* of my clients made money in 2008 by following my financial advice, and some earned as much as a 20% positive return. How did your portfolio fare? If you didn't earn a positive return on your accounts and you want to turn that around, this book and The Trinity Plan is for you. We also pray for, and with, our clients. We put God at the center of the work we do, and we thank Him for the opportunity to help you.

Over the past couple of years, millions of people have tuned in to listen to my financial advice on the radio and television. During that time, many people have lost as much as 60% of the value in their investment portfolio, but the people who listened to and acted upon my advice have cut their losses, and began to make money. You may ask, How can people make money at a time when so many are losing over half of their investments and retirement accounts?

＊ It all depends on how you view, and use money; or do you worship money, by placing the value of your money over your value of God? This book will outline how you can join my clients in making money while your neighbors follow the same old path with the masses who blindly adhere to the "one-size-fits-all" approach.

When you were a child and did something just because your friend did it first, remember your Mom asking, "If all your friends jumped off a cliff, would you do that, too?" That's the mentality that is leading this economic disaster we are witnessing in our nation today. **Our government is spending money that we don't have to prop up companies that by all estimates should be allowed to fail.** Many people are following the advice of those who want everyone to jump off the same cliff, and like sheep following each other, they're falling off into economic destruction.   This book can help you break this cycle.

"Too big to fail" seems to be the buzzword today, whether we're talking about lending institutions, car manufacturers, or investment companies. It seems like everyone is trying to get all the money they can from what you and I pay in taxes. And some economists are saying that we haven't seen the worst of this mess yet.

Recently I heard an economist on a financial network say that the stock market will likely rise for awhile, but as soon as people start seeing a little bit of what they lost over the past year begin to come back – they'll pull everything out again.

According to his report, this mass exodus could drive our current recession into a depression. I don't even want to think about what would happen if we had another terrorist attack on our soil. Our government is spending money that we don't have to prop up companies that by all estimates *should* be allowed to fail, with no guarantee of their future survivability.

It's like a young man going to his Dad to co-sign a loan for a new car that the boy really can't afford. When the bank calls to collect the three months of past due payments the son couldn't make, who has to pay the bill? That's right, dear old Dad is stuck with the bill that must be paid to protect his own credit score.

Now imagine that same Dad with hundreds of kids he has co-signed for that can't make their payments, and all the bills are being presented for payment to him in the amount of trillions of dollars at the same time. Dad in this case is the U.S. government, and the kids are the companies bellying up to the "TARP" (Troubled Asset Relief Program) counter looking for free money.

But what happens when Dad can't pay the bill either? The whole family ends up filing bankruptcy. Is that what we are, a nation that bankrupts itself, instead of allowing one of the kids to fail and possibly learn a lesson from it? The other kids would have also learned a valuable lesson from their sibling's failure.

Don't think that nations can't fail when they are improperly managed. Remember Venice, Egypt, The Ottoman Empire, and Rome, once called the greatest civilization on earth? History has a way of repeating itself. This isn't a prophecy, but an observation.

Savings Thought

Want to save money when you eat out? Instead of ordering soft drinks, coffee or tea, ask for a glass of water only. You will save from $1.50 to $3.00 per person! A family of four following this advice could save as much as $1,872 per year, and be much healthier!

How will you protect yourself from the potentially negative impact that this economic situation, or "money storm," could have on families – and especially your family – in our country? How will your portfolio survive or overcome such difficulties? You have one of two choices:

» Continue following the advice sold to the masses, which has everyone doing the same thing in a "one-size-fits-all" approach to planning; or,

» Allow Christian financial professionals who volunteer their time through our ministry to design a financial plan specifically for your family.

This book discusses how the second choice can help you survive economically challenging situations that I call "money storms," and also be poised to recognize and take advantage of financial opportunities when they avail themselves. The "Trinity Plan" is that beam of hope for you during those storms.

Determining how we utilize money must be done the same way we determine how we use our time, talents, and other assets. Would you give someone the use of your car if you weren't positive they would bring it back in the same, or better, shape that it was in when you lent it to them?

Then why do we allow others to take our money without knowing in what condition they will return it?

Today millions of consumers have to deal with credit card problems, outrageously high car payments, and adjustable rate mortgages where they owe more to the bank than the home is even worth. There are problems facing people today not seen since the Great Depression.

These certainly are stormy times, and families need, more than ever, a ray or beam of hope that can guide them, not just through these stormy times but through the rebuilding times that will follow.

Getting out of debt is a basic principle. You either have to spend less, or make more money. It's that simple. I know there are people who sell books with formulas to get this done, but the bottom line is you have to make more or spend less. In addition to our ministry, a good source of help for debt situations is Crown Financial Ministry. You can learn more about them at www.crown.org.

Dave Ramsey and other entertainers understand how to deal with debt and debt-related issues. I don't agree with them on very much, but Ramsey's methods of dealing with debt have helped many people across the country. Beyond that, he tries to sell a "one-size-fits-all" philosophy to financial planning, which is in direct opposition to what those of us who are actually licensed and trained on such issues believe and use every day in our successful practices!

You will notice I repeatedly refer to these folks offering their cookie cutter, and do it yourself approaches to finance as entertainers throughout this book. I label them as such because to my knowledge, many of them have no valid licenses to discuss the topics of investing or insurance. We'll discuss the importance of these licenses later in this book.

Everyone's situation, goals, and ambitions are different, and should be treated as such. One prime example of where we differ in philosophy is mortgages. Dave says to obtain a 15-year mortgage, and then send the bank everything you can to get it paid off early.

That may not sound like a bad idea, but let me ask you this. You get a 15-year mortgage. Making your payments is a struggle for you, but you decide the struggle is worth it to have your home paid off early.

Now if you lose your job, someone in your family gets sick or other expenses, such as food or gas, increase and make it impossible for you to pay your mortgage on time, what happens? Your mortgage is almost double what it could have been if you had obligated yourself to a lower payment through a 30-year mortgage.

Another question: Do you have access to all that equity in case you need it to pay bills? No, you have to apply for a loan from the bank in the form of a home equity line of credit (HELOC), or home equity loan.

But you can't qualify for the loan because you have lost your job, and you're paying your bills late, if you can pay them at all. Now you're getting hits on your credit score, so eventually you'll fall behind several payments and face foreclosure.

What if, instead, you had obtained a 30 year mortgage which would have reduced your monthly obligation to the bank? Some people say then send extra money to your bank to pay off the mortgage, but I say don't!

I say set up an account that will earn you compound interest and send your money there. You can still decide to use that money to pay your home off early if you want, but by following my advice you will have accomplished four things:

1. You have control over your money (instead of giving it to the bank).
2. You create a safety net to help you weather the financial storms when they come.
3. You are on the right track to obtain financial independence!
4. You'll enjoy an abundant life because you have access to your money without having to apply for a loan to get it.

I know this may seem like radical thinking. I mean really, who actually has any money that they can get to today? Remember, you are doing the same thing that you were going to do by sending extra money to your mortgage company, you just send it to an account that you have control over. You can still let it sit there and earn interest for 15 years then write a check to the bank and live debt free, but you do it in your own time frame, not someone else's.

The only difference – and it's a big difference – is that if hard times come if you lose your job, or there's an illness in the family, you don't have to go to the bank and ask to borrow any of your own money, and then run the risk of getting denied the loan which will multiply the negative effects of everything else going on in your life at that time. You use your safety net money wisely until help arrives. People who have access to, and control over their money will always prevail during challenging economic times!

Another example I would like to briefly point out is our perception of 401K, which is only a *supplemental* retirement plan, not the foundation that so many have come to depend on for their financial future. I recently read an article in the March 2009 edition of Money Magazine about 401(k) plans. I was shocked to see that someone finally came out and agreed with what I've been saying for years.

On page 11 in this issue the editor's note states, "What the market crash revealed is that this 25-year experiment in retirement savings, originally designed as a way for high earners to shelter a bit of income from taxes, is in serious need of serious reform." The writer goes on to say, "The 401(k) does little or nothing for the majority of workers who aren't covered or get no matching contribution from their employers or are in a tax bracket where the tax deferral simply doesn't mean much."

More and more today we are finding fewer employers matching employee contributions to 401(k) plans. With employers cutting their contributions, the employee's 401(k) plans become absolutely useless. We'll talk more about this in a later chapter

I have been preaching against the grain about this for years, but I didn't have a loud enough voice. I hate that it took one of the hardest financial lessons in American history to get someone to finally come out and say this in a nationally recognized publication. This "experiment" cost a lot of good people huge amounts of money, and in some cases their entire retirement dreams. You will hear about my thoughts on retirement planning later in this book.

Throughout the rest of this book you will be exposed to truths that banks, insurance companies, and others do not want you to hear. You will learn secrets that the wealthiest people use every day to multiply their assets in an effort to keep the rest of us wondering how they do it.

Companies have invested billions of dollars in advertising and sponsorship programs to train you to think the way they want you to think. Now we are going to blow the lid off some of this information in an effort to enrich you with knowledge, encourage you with confidence, and empower you with truth. So if you're ready for the inside scoop, let's move on.

Chapter Two

Your Pathway to Success: Introducing the D.E.C.M. Principle

I once heard my favorite author, Dr. John C. Maxwell, one of the most influential and respected leadership teachers in the business world, say that a man can live 40 days without food, four days without water, four minutes without air, but only four seconds without hope. When you are dedicated to improving any situation in your life, you must have hope that it can be accomplished. When you are filled with hope, and the Holy Spirit, there is nothing you can't do. You may fall short of your goals, but you will inevitably improve because of the experience.

Let's take a look at something that will help you improve in all aspects of your life, with particular attention to your finances.

God revealed this information to me a few years ago, but I didn't understand how He wanted me to implement it. That idea is the **D.E.C.M. Principle**.

In order to succeed at anything in life, there are four elements that have to be present and addressed effectively to ensure optimum results. It doesn't matter if you are preparing for a test in school, hoping for a promotion at work, or committing to a change in your financial situation. If you apply these elements, and are determined to improve that situation, you will not fail!

The four elements are *Dedication*, *Education*, *Communication*, and *Motivation*. These elements are the foundation that every person who has ever accomplished anything in life has embraced, and utilized effectively to reach whatever level of success they've achieved. We will address and explain each of the four elements and how they relate to money, or the way we look at it. If you will apply this principle to various other aspects of your life, you probably will be able to apply it to your finances very easily.

The first element in the D.E.C.M. principle: DEDICATION

Dedication is a firm commitment to a person, cause, organization, idea or issue that typically involves unwavering persistence to a positive and rewarding outcome. When people see "the vision," it helps them to be dedicated and to continue diligently working for that desired outcome.

> "The first rule is not to lose. The second rule is not to forget the first rule."
> —Warren Buffet

As we discuss this element, I want to ensure you that the program I am laying out for you allows you to constantly keep in view your desired results. This will allow you to keep your eyes on the finish line and will help guide you and keep you focused on where your dedication is as well as where it should be.

You can only drift away from your dedicated task or goal if you allow yourself to become distracted with no way to re-focus your actions. Keep in mind that obstacles and challenges will constantly get in your way and will serve to distract you, and take you down a different path. Expecting these obstacles will help you prevent and combat them.

Some obstacles that you will undoubtedly witness are:

1. Peer pressure to venture away from a godly view of finances
2. A desire to invest in a "get rich quick" scheme
3. Swayed by unqualified theories from entertainers on radio or television
4. Temptations to purchase items that do not bring glory to God, or a positive situation at home
5. Unnecessary stress and worry

When you face these or other distractions, simply remember that with God all things are possible!

Let's take a look at where your dedication is right now.

I have heard it said that if you show me your checkbook, I'll show you where your dedication is. There is a lot of truth to that statement. I have an

> The difference between average people and successful people is their perception of, and reaction to, failure.
> —Dr. John C. Maxwell
> *Failing Forward*

exercise that I would like to share with you to help you effectively utilize this element.

Open your checkbook or bank statement and, with a pink or red highlighter, mark the expenditures that were made for self gratification. This includes; going out to eat; movies and other entertainment; new clothes; renting or purchasing video games and related equipment and materials; and credit card payments.

With a yellow highlighter, mark your fixed expenses such as utilities, car payments, mortgage payment, and insurances.

Now with a green highlighter, mark your contributions to church, donations made to Christian organizations, and money you gave to the needy.

Just take a look at the amount of red on your ledger sheet. You see all the discretionary money that is going out each month? The color covering the most area is where your dedication is right now. Is that where you want it to be? If not, we need to think about a change.

Here is a little something I would like you to think about as we go through this D.E.C.M. Principle:

*Dedication creates a desire to become better educated. Education is strength. Communicating with others increases your abilities and opportunities, producing motivation. Motivation gets things and people moving. A dedicated person with an educated motivation who communicates their thoughts effectively, brings forth appropriate action. Appropriate actions produce **positive results**.*

"I don't do things half-heartedly. Because I know if I do, then I can expect half-hearted results."
—Michael Jordan

If you are not happy with where you are financially, and want the situation to improve, the first thing that has to occur is that you must be willing to change some things. These things will be different for each one of us, but change has to happen. For the person drowning in credit card debt, change might be behavioral in nature.

When you feel the urge to break out the plastic, do something else instead like take a long walk, or sit down and write out the reasons you shouldn't make that purchase, or volunteer to do something that will help someone else. Nothing will change your attitude toward your own problems faster than helping someone with worse problems that your own.

> "God will never bring you to anything that He won't bring you through."

For the person having difficulty sleeping at night because they are so worried about their retirement money and how much they are losing in the stock market, they might need to move their money into a safer environment where they are earning interest instead of having their funds in such a volatile situation. No matter what we want to accomplish, the first step usually involves some type of change. I don't remember where I heard it, but a great acronym for change is:

Come

Have

A

New

Growth

Experience

Are you listening to encouragers regularly? If not, remove yourself from those who seek to keep status quo, and find others who want to excel in life through Christ. If you encourage someone, they will encourage you in return. Then you can go back and become an encouragement to those who used to be discouraging toward you, and give them hope. Changing the way you view things will change the way you are viewed! We can never change the world if we don't start by changing ourselves first.

I have found in my own life, as well as offering advice to others for the past 17 years in the financial services industry, that this recipe is one for success in all aspects of our lives, not just money. But when applied to our faith and our money together, great things can occur. Our *dedication* to anything is the most crucial element of the four.

• One such example of dedication is Hernando Cortes, a Spanish explorer in the sixteenth century. He and his team of 600 Spanish soldiers landed in Mexico to conquer the Aztec nation. The battles would pit 600 Spaniards against 5 million Aztec people, not very good odds. In an effort to prevent any of his team from considering retreat, Cortes set fire to all of his ships. There was no choice. They had to complete the task at hand. Now that's dedication!

• Maybe we should burn the ships that brought us to where we are financially and address the fight ahead of us against our own financial enemy wholeheartedly. No matter how many problems or failures you have faced in the past that brought you to this point, you have to look at these failures as learning experiences.

One book I would recommend to everyone is "Failing Forward," by John C. Maxwell. (Published by Thomas Nelson Inc.) This book played a significant role in changing my life by teaching me how to deal with failures. Failing at anything is nothing to be ashamed of, if you learn from it, and adjust future actions accordingly.

Dedication is that point where you say, OK, I've messed up, but I'm not going to let that get me down or stop me from trying to be successful. Remember that success is a journey, not a destination. No one will announce, like on a train, "Next stop success!" If you've been waiting to hear that announcement, I'm sorry to burst your bubble.

If we are dedicated to being the best we can be, we must first see where our daily dedications are placed, and ask ourselves if we are truly dedicated to serving God first. The two places you will find this information is in your calendar and the register page of your checkbook.

If we don't schedule our time effectively, we'll be wandering aimlessly with no direction. The same is true for our money. We'll ask ourselves, where did it all go? I had plenty yesterday. You need to track the money you spend by noting it in your checkbook, a legal pad, or on a computer program. What, you say you don't currently track your time or money? We may have just found your level of dedication. That didn't take long! If that's you, start here.

Begin tracking every hour of your day using the God's Dollar calendar. You also need to document every dime you spend in your checkbook, The God's Dollar Money Tracker, a legal pad, or on a computer program, but somehow document where your money is going, and for what purpose. Once we determine where your time is spent, and where the money goes, we can begin seeing to what things or ideas you are actually dedicated. **Caution**: this might not be pretty!

You can find free resources for this exercise on our website at www. godsdollar.com, or by calling my office at 252-809-1883. I'll make sure you get whatever resources you need. Contact information is on our website. I've also enclosed budgeting and tracking forms to our website for your convenience.

When I think of dedication I think of people committed to a cause so important that they would die to protect it. That would be our dedication to our family, right? Do you have that same dedication to your faith? Are you dedicated to tithing 10 percent of your income

because you want to give back to God a portion of that with which
He has blessed you, or do you hold on to that because things are just
a little tight right now? Have you ever said He'll understand because
God knows how bad our situation is?

If that's the case, were you truly committed to God or to worldly bills
you felt needed to be paid first? I know that's a painful thing. I've been
there more times than I would like to admit, but when you lovingly give
from your first fruits, God rewards you with more every time. **You can
never outgive God!** If you don't believe me, try Him. Give faithfully
with a loving heart, not expecting anything in return, except to be a
blessing. You'll find that the more you bless others, the more you will
be blessed. This does take dedication, but might be the first in a series
of changes that will eventually set you free of financial struggles.

The second element we need to discuss is EDUCATION:

In II Chronicles 17:7-9 we learn that King Jehoshaphat was so
committed to properly educating the children in his kingdom that he
sent out priests, Levites and his officials to travel to all the towns of Judah
to educate everyone in the word of God. In the New Living Translation
verse 9 says, *"They took copies of the "Book of the Law of the Lord" and traveled
around through all the towns of Judah, teaching the people."*

Jehoshaphat knew that he must make sure people were educated
in the word of God, or they would be vulnerable to the influence
of the enemy. He realized that the only hope his kingdom had for
continued prosperity was to provide a good education in the things
that mattered most, godly knowledge to the people who would need
them in life. (It's ashamed that so many public school systems in
America do not share that same Christian education philosophy)

I love what Mark Twain said about education. He said, "I'll never let schooling interfere with my education". He understood that we should never stop learning. He also realized that what we learn through structured education in a teaching environment is not all we need. Without real life experiences, we would be ignorant of almost everything important to the survival of our species. I guarantee that you'll never hear about "The Hundred Year Test" in a schoolroom.

God revealed this idea to me several years ago as a tool to measure the importance of every issue we will ever face individually, or as a society. Here's how it works. Take an issue like the debate over whether or not eggs are good for you. There has been conflicting information on this issue for decades both for eating more eggs and not eating them at all. Let's just say that everyone in the world decided to not eat any eggs for 100 years.

"Education's purpose is to replace an empty mind with an open one."
—Malcolm Forbes

What impact would this have on the human race 100 years from now? There would be no difference except for the fact we would all be tired of pancakes or waffles for breakfast every day.

Apply this test to issues that are important to you. You will be amazed at the potential results. There are some issues I'd love to bring up to you that I've applied this test to, but that's for another book.

I encourage everyone to read, study, and listen to all aspects of finance, and not just take my word for things. Unlike some authors, I try to keep an open mind about things, unless they are in direct conflict with God's word.

Now let me clarify, though. I do not consider water cooler talk to be educational when it comes to personal finance. A lot of people are led astray by listening to what their co-worker told them about the tremendous success they had following one program or another. Have you ever known someone who was quick to share their limitations or failures with you, or just the good things?

Your friend Andy at the office may have hit it big in the stock market buying 500 shares of Widget Company USA. He might have made a profit of 500% last week. After hearing this, you buy 200 shares at the current price, but something happens in the distribution cycle of their widgets and the stock plummets. Andy says he sure is glad he got out the day before, but you're sitting there with worthless widget stock. Is your co-worker accountable to you for your losses? Not legally, but did you get an education? You bet you did! Anything in life that makes us feel angry, sad, happy or guilty is typically an education that no teaching institution can ever provide.

When a person with experience meets a person with money, the person with the money usually ends up gaining experience, and the one with experience ends up gaining the money.

These life lessons are ones that stick with us. These are experiences that we either want to know again, so we duplicate the type of events that caused the euphoric feelings, or experiences that we never want to know again so we train our minds to be aware of warning signs that might cause us to fall into the same old traps. Remember that God allows us to experience trials and tribulations in an effort to strengthen us for His service. Just like iron is forged in a furnace to make it stronger, so to God's people are forged to make us stronger servants for Him. *God will never bring you to anything that He will not bring you through.*

A warning sign of debt-related issues might be when we have just reduced or eliminated our servitude to a creditor and feel free to enjoy life again. Then we pull out the plastic and invite 10 of our closest friends to the nicest steakhouse in town to celebrate with us. The desire to do that should be a warning of impending danger of falling right back into the same old trap that got us there to begin with.

A better idea might be to have these same friends over to your home for a potluck dinner where everyone brings a covered dish. Everyone will appreciate the relaxed atmosphere, and have a great time enjoying food that they know they'll like. After all, are they celebrating you and your accomplishment, or the debt that caused you so much pain? You will be a better example to them, and a better witness of good stewardship by celebrating this way. The way you handle situations like this will demonstrate a true education from the school of real life.

I would like to share with you the part of my "real life" education that means more to me than any letters after my name from educational institutions:

✳ *I've earned the equivalent of a Bachelor's degree in procrastination, a Master's degree in poor decision making, and a Ph.D in "failurology". All of this, though, has been capped off with an honorary Doctorate in forgiveness from Mercy University, which was presented to me personally by the Dean of the school, God. Every bit of this education was made possible through a scholarship paid for by my savior Jesus Christ.*

The third element in the D.E.C.M. principle is COMMUNICATION.

Communicating with others who have endured and persevered through problems similar to yours is crucial, and often encouraging! It doesn't matter what situation or difficulty you are going through.

When you understand that you are not the only one who is going, or has ever gone through it, or who has survived situations like yours or worse, makes it easier to overcome. Naturally I turn to the book of Job in the Bible to see that whatever problems I'm dealing with is nothing compared to what Job went through, and yet praised God for.

When God restored Job (Job 42:10-17) to greater wealth and prosperity than he had before his trials, He saw that his faith was enough to see him through. Before Job's restoration, some of his friends came to talk to him about his plight. They accused him of being guilty of sin, and bringing all of his problems upon himself. Job remained faithful, and continued to communicate with God by praying for those who condemned him, praising Him through everything. Job's decision to listen to and believe God and not to the criticism of his

I Peter 1:15
"But as he which hath called you is holy, so be ye holy in all manner of communication."
—KJV

friends is the only reason he was able to prevail among the negativity of those around him.

Encouraging and truthful communication is crucial, especially when communicating with God. Always surround yourself with people who can help you overcome issues, not those who want you to succumb to them. If you're dealing with financial issues that are getting you down, turn to the Bible first! Then seek Christian professional assistance. One such place to find that encouragement is through our ministry. You could also listen to encouraging and uplifting music, such as that played on many contemporary Christian radio stations.

If we think of communication as a well-planned and maintained superhighway system, we get the picture that ideas and thoughts can travel from one point to another and back again without delay. But what happens when there is an accident or road construction that changes the normal flow of traffic? What if the detour signs all pointed in the wrong direction? What if they were all printed in a foreign language that we couldn't understand? Our superhighway would become a super parking lot. No one would want to travel, and if they did there would be no guarantee that they would safely get to where they were going. It would be a confusing mess!

Unfortunately that's what communication has become for too many of us. We think we are providing the mechanism to allow for smooth and safe travel of our ideas, but they get detoured or totally lost because of bad directions or poor execution. What if every time you tried to communicate, your message was lost or misunderstood, would you even want to keep trying? What if you were expecting a positive and uplifting message, but instead you were met with a barrage of negativity and complaints? Would you want to stick around to hear more?

If people would learn to communicate more effectively, relationships would be saved and new ones built, especially the most important relationship, the one between you and God. In an effort to repair our potentially broken communication highway, we must start with knowing how to effectively communicate with God. This will be addressed in detail in a later chapter.

One important thing to remember when communicating with others about your finances is to make sure you are listening to someone who knows what they are talking about, and not people who are just trying to make you think they do. Be careful of wolves in sheep's clothing!

One sure way to make sure your advice comes from someone reliable is to ask what state or federal licenses they hold that enables them to offer such advice. All true financial professionals hold valid licenses to operate issued by either State or Federal agencies or both.

If they have none, they also have no one to be accountable to if they give you bad advice.

You should always control the first part of your communication, not the one wanting you to follow them or their thoughts.

Before the introduction of GPS devices, I remember having to stop and ask directions when on trips to areas I'd never been before. Yes, I am the exception to the rule of men not stopping to ask directions. One thing I would make sure of is that I was talking with someone who lived in the area in which I was trying to get directions. I felt that I would get better advice from someone who actually knew the roads over someone like me who just thought they knew.

II Timothy 5:8
"But if any not provide for his own, and especially for those of his own house, he hath denied the faith and is worse than an infidel."
—KJV

I remember back when I was a boy growing up at the beach. Tourists would come up to us as we were carrying our surfboards and ask us which way the ocean was from where we were. Some of my friends thought it funny to offer up directions to Stumpy Point, a small fishing village about 50 miles inland of where they wanted to be. We all laughed at the thought that these ignorant people were about a block away from the Atlantic Ocean, but would drive so far out of the way because they were told to. We thought it funny because we didn't have to be accountable to anyone for what we said.

Of course not everyone gives poor advice in an intentionally malicious attempt to make someone else feel stupid, but poor advice is poor advice no matter the intent behind it. If you were one of these folks my friends mislead, I'm truly sorry! This is one of those examples of education for the ones being led astray as well as for those of us doing the leading. Guilt will be one reason I would never offer poor advice to anyone, partially because of this story.

Communication can obviously be used for good and for evil. We have the sole responsibility to decide whether or not to listen to that information and act upon it. You naturally increase the likelihood of receiving accurate information when you first learn that the person offering it is accountable to someone else, like a State licensing board or commission, for what they are telling you.

The final element for success is MOTIVATION:

If you are dedicated to a Christian lifestyle and following the examples of so many before us, your motivation is to serve God honorably, and be the best witness possible to others. The primary scripture I turn to about this accountability is Matthew 25:14-30, I hope you will read it for yourself, but to summarize: In this scripture Jesus tells the parable of the three servants given gifts according to their abilities to use while their master is away. Upon the return of the master they are all commanded to give an accounting of how they used those gifts, and the results. Both of the first two servants told the master that they had doubled that which was entrusted to them. The master responded by saying, "Well done my good and faithful servant." The third servant buried his gifts and

"I believe that if you show people the problems and you show them the solutions, they will be moved to act."
—Bill Gates

didn't use them at all. He brought them back to the master just as they had been entrusted to him. The master then said to the third, "You wicked and lazy servant I cast you out into the darkness and gnashing of teeth. You could have at least earned interest on my money."

If we want to do the best we can with what has been entrusted to us, we might be motivated by pleasing the one who entrusted these things to us to begin with. But even if your motivation is to simply provide for your family the Bible gives us instructions to do that too. II Timothy 5:8 says, *"But if any not provide for his own, and especially for those of his own house, he hath denied the faith and is worse than an infidel."*

When I think of motivation, I also think of the engine of a freight train, especially the steam engines of the nineteenth century. When you realize the incredible weight of what these engines used to pull for hundreds of miles, it is mind boggling. We will discuss specific motivational factors later in this book.

Operation Lifesaver, a train safety program sponsored by federal, state, and local governments, says that a typical freight train weighs approximately 8,000 tons, or 16 million pounds. How do you get that much weight moving in the direction you want it to go? Different types of engines have hauled that massive amount of steel and cargo for generations, but the one I want you to think about is steam.

Steam produces enough energy to cause as much as 16 million pounds of mass to move as fast as 70 miles per hour. But the smallest detail could prevent that train from ever moving one inch. If the water did not reach 212 degrees Fahrenheit, the water wouldn't boil and no steam would be created. Think about it: All that water at 211 degrees is just a hot mass of liquid, but heating by just one more degree creates energy enough to move that iron and steel along with all its cargo. That one extra degree is the level of motivation it took to cause the engine to be able to work properly and effectively.

What is your level of motivation? Do you need to bump up the temperature one degree or 100 degrees, and how will you do it? What difference would that make in your life?

Let's sum up what we've learned in this chapter.

1. Find out what you are dedicated to by determining where you spend your money and your time.

2. The level of dedication we put into something will determine the level of results we receive from our efforts.

3. Remember that obstacles will challenge your dedication and commitment to God. You have to be prepared to face difficulties and challenges every day.

4. In order to achieve different results, we have to **CHANGE** certain habits or attitudes.

5. Only listen to people who will suffer consequences if they offer bad advice.

6. You should always demand credentials when people offer financial advice.

7. Do business with people who seek to educate you, not those who just say "Do it my way".

8. You can never out give God!

9. We must remove ourselves from negative attitudes, and those who are not actively helping us succeed. We can then return to offer help to those who were not encouraging before.

10. Find encouragement through people, books you read and the music to which you are listening.

11. Communicate with people who seek God's will above their own.

12. We'll have to offer an accounting one day of how we used God's gifts. How will you respond?

13. Find what motivates you to make positive changes in your life.

14. Add the necessary effort that will allow you to see your desired results.

Remember that as long as you keep doing the same things you've done, you will obtain the same level of results you have. If you were happy with those results, you wouldn't be reading this book. Together, and with God's guidance we can change your results by changing the behavior or attitude that caused them.

In the next chapter, we're going to discuss some differences between my method of financial planning and others that are so prevalent in our society today, and the motivating factors behind those myths. Understanding why some people say and do the things they do, will give you a better understanding of why it is so important to change the opinions to which you are listening.

Also, in the next chapter, I'm going to show you some people and information to look out for that may prevent you from making some painful mistakes. I'll also introduce you to some folks just like you who were looking for help that fell into these traps before they met me. I hope their stories will help you avoid the pain and anguish some of these people endured.

Chapter Three

Do We Really Need *Another* Book About Finance?

$

It has been difficult for me to write a book about finance, because I have always told people that they should turn to Christian professionals for counsel about their specific financial situation. We should not fall prey to any "one-size-fits-all" approach that people typically sell us through some books. In fact, I stated on The American Family Radio Network (AFR), and on television, on CBN (Christian Broadcasting Network), that people should always turn to the Bible for the truth about how to handle money, not worldly books.

I also knew that my life in the past certainly had not been a perfect example of how to use money, (although maybe the

> God doesn't always call the qualified, but He always qualifies the called.

perfect example of how *not* to use money). I'll explain in detail what I'm talking about later, but just know I've made some HUGE mistakes in the past that almost prevented me from writing this book.

Thankfully I listen to my own advice now, and things are going well. I asked God and some of my friends how I could justify telling people how to effectively use money when I have messed up so badly on my own. I heard the words "God doesn't always call the qualified, but He always qualifies the called".

Through the lessons I've learned from mistakes I've made, and have helped others overcome, I know God has qualified me. There is no doubt that He has called me to bring to you this message of hope. Someone has to start telling people the truth and not just selling the same old stale ideas that are causing our country to slide into financial ruin.

Did you realize that our country would not have needed a $700,000,000,000 ($700 billion) bailout in 2008 if so many innocent people had not placed their life savings in the stock market through investment plans at the advice of people on radio and television? In fact, many of my colleagues and I have discussed this trend for several years. I'll give you some examples of our discussions.

We are constantly amazed at the number of people who think that the only way to build wealth is to buy mutual funds through their retirement plans or college savings plans. Hundreds of billions, if not more, dollars were needlessly lost in these accounts during the financial meltdown of 2008. In fact, if the free market system would have worked the way it was supposed to, some companies would have gone bankrupt because of bad business decisions, and some people would have lost their jobs, but not nearly to the magnitude we saw during that time period.

Wall Street would have suffered, and some economic struggles would have occurred. People like you and me though, who are just trying to provide a living for our families, would not have seen the almost catastrophic fallout that we witnessed. We wouldn't suffer if we knew which advice we could trust.

Example One:

I heard an interview with a famous television personality who gives financial advice on TV some time back, in December 2008 or January 2009. She always tells people to send their money to the stock market because you can't get that kind of return anywhere else. I'm glad I don't get that kind of return where my money is, because I would have been like many Americans in 2008 and lost 40% or more of my holdings.

Anyway, this particular entertainer was asked where she puts her money during these economically challenged times. She told the reporter that her money was in bonds, not the stock market.

Later that week I was flipping through channels and heard her tell yet another person to have faith in the system, and let the money stay there because the market will rebound, and keep contributing to your employer's supplemental retirement plan. I refer to 401(k) plans as supplemental retirement accounts because they were never designed to be a primary retirement plan. I'll explain more later in this book.

> "The 401(k) does little or nothing for the majority of workers who aren't covered or get no matching contribution from their employers or are in a bracket where the tax deferral simply doesn't mean much."
> —*Money Magazine* (March 2009)

This is the type of hypocrisy we need to be turned away from. But what do we turn to? We just get more of the same old stuff from a different teacher because there has been no one with a national voice to tell us anything different, until now.

U.S. Rep. **George Miller**, chairman of the House Education and Labor Committee said on October 7, 2008 that American workers currently had approximately $3 trillion in 401(k) plans invested in equity products such as mutual funds.

To put this into perspective for you, if you were born the same day as Jesus Christ, and spent $1 million dollars per day until right now you still couldn't have spent $1 trillion. Who has a calculator with trillions anyway? Now multiply that amount three times. Are you beginning to understand why Congress needed to pass a "bailout"?

I believe that it wasn't to protect businesses as much as the workers with their life savings tied to "the market". Of course, if they had announced this information, everyone would have immediately pulled their money out of their retirement plans and caused a whole different basket of problems.

Financial challenges always occur when you give up control of and access to your money, and give it to others with a promise of return with no guarantee. We'll talk about this in depth in a later chapter though.

BEWARE of "Get Rich Quick Schemes", but be more careful of those who have fallen prey to them, and now want to show how they can help you!

For years I have witnessed first-hand the devastation to families that is caused by financial issues. I have seen these problems in the lives and relationships of families

I have tried to help, and I have seen it in my own life and personal relationships.

It doesn't matter whether you have too much month left at the end of your money, or you have an abundance of assets. The way we view, use and sometimes worship money is the underlying issue that will tear a family apart faster than any other problem we face today. Because of my personal experience, and the fact that so many people are falling prey to entertainers giving financial advice that they are not licensed or trained to offer, I feel that I have an obligation to share these pages with you. Allow me to share some stories with you about what I've seen that had a direct impact upon me writing this book.

I was asked to work with the employees of a large corporation some time ago. The employer had a counselor who had attended a four-day certification class sponsored by one of these entertainers come in and "help" their employees about a year earlier.

Now don't get me wrong, this particular entertainer offered some good advice about eliminating debt, but he is not licensed to conduct business in the financial services industry as of the date I am writing this book. Nor was he licensed to do so when he or his un-licensed representative offered the advice I'm about to share with you.

Now that you realize that there are people offering this one-size-fits-all advice who really shouldn't be allowed to legally conduct this type of business, let me give you an example of why they shouldn't be permitted to operate without a license or some kind of accountability.

Example Two:

I met with a young lady some time ago. We'll call her Grace. Grace had listened to the advice from one of these so-called counselors. She was told that she should cash in the two life insurance policies that she and her husband owned, which were both earning a decent rate of interest for them. Grace followed through with the advice. Grace was excited about cashing in the two policies and receiving the cash value, which was equal to about $7,000. Then she planned to pay off some debt and invest the remainder of that money in the stock market, where she was told it would grow by at least 12%.

You may ask; Was she actually told this? Yes she was, and with no ramifications to the ones telling her this. In fact at one time the radio personality that offered this class to the counselor used to have a video on his website that showed people that if they invested their money in mutual funds they would get an average of 12% return, and thereby create a fund with which they could use to purchase new cars every so many years.

Savings Thought

Instead of buying a new car and making payments after you buy it, what if you save money to replace the engine or other major parts of a vehicle you own? Buy a new car for $30,000 or replace engine for $2,500 to $4,000?

That's another tidbit that these people like to sell you. Since I hold three different securities licenses (including one that allows me to supervise other financial advisors), if I told people they could get a 12% return by investing in any mutual fund, the Securities and Exchange Commission (SEC) would lock me up under the jail and throw away the key.

Anyway, after following this advice, Grace was quite disturbed to learn that the cash value of the life insurance policy was almost completely eliminated by fees and surrender charges. These fees and charges occur when you surrender the policy early. If they had needed the money without surrendering it, they could have accessed funds without these penalties and fees. That's where a licensed specialist comes in handy.

Since they had purchased the original life insurance, something else amazing had happened: They both had grown older than when they had purchased the policies, making the cost of new term insurance more expensive to purchase.

The $7,000 that Grace thought she was going to be able to use to pay off debt and invest had been reduced to around $2,000, and the cost of the term life insurance that they had been instructed to purchase cost more than the "counselor" had told them.

You see, that counselor had no way of accurately quoting insurance rates because he/she wasn't licensed with any state or appointed with any company to do so.

They were simply reading from the "one-size-fits-all" script that someone sold them from their "business in a box". What Grace did accomplish was to throw away approximately $5,000, cause great difficulty in her marriage, and pay for the bad advice they received from this counselor.

This entertainer I mentioned earlier tells attendees of his "certification classes" that they can charge up to $1,195 for a two-to-four hour counseling session where they offer the same old stale advice to buy term life insurance and invest the rest.

This is a simple message to teach people to regurgitate, and this makes it easy to get people to buy a "business in a box". Some of the people who go to churches and play this

Professionals who have worked hard for years to earn licenses and industry certifications will be much more likely to have the answers that will be in your best interest.

entertainer's DVD, then schedule follow up sessions with attendees, may have been working at a Jiffy Lube last week, or cleaning rooms at the local Holiday Inn. Is this the experience you want to trust your financial future to?

Folks, as a trained, licensed, and experienced financial advisor, I can't charge someone $1,195 for a two-to-four hour session, and then sleep at night. I especially wouldn't be able to sleep if I knew that the reason I was meeting with these people to begin with was because they are already having financial difficulties.

Situations like these are why I started The Abundant Life Institute, to offer people a place to find trusted Christian professionals who will give of their time to help others. You don't need to pay anyone for advice any longer, especially not for bad advice.

The problems Grace and her family faced are not isolated. More times than I can count, I have gone behind these "counselors" and people who just try to follow the basic "buy term and invest the rest" mantra that has been drilled into our minds since the 1970s.

Life insurance companies love this "buy term" idea because statistics show that less than 15% of all term life insurance sold in America ever has to pay a death claim. That's 85% of all term life insurance policies and premiums, which translate into clear profit for the insurance companies.

When billions of dollars are spent to cause us to think a certain way, the people who want us to think that way make sure we don't hear anything but what they want us to.

Voices like mine are all over this country, but very few have the opportunity or the courage to go against the company who might be paying their salary or commissions. So we just keep quiet, and share our thoughts with one person at a time, and try to make a difference for those who will listen with an open mind.

Do We Really Need Another Book About Finance? 49

After all, we show people:

> » Everybody's situation is different.
> » We all got to where we are through a variety of ways and through different situations that took different time periods.
> » Even though we all want to save money, we all have different needs, and ways we are comfortable going about it.
> » Some people want to make sure they have enough money to pay for their children's college
> » We all have different interests and needs to prepare for in our retirement years.
> » We all have different needs now that may require access to different amounts of money.
> » Some of us have elderly parents we help care for, or one day will care for.
> » Not everyone will be able to buy life insurance after their 10 or 20 year term policy comes up for renewal because of health issues, or affordability.

Example Three:

There is another potential pitfall that you need to be made aware of. A company that advertises a method of paying down your mortgage which will allow you to pay your house off in just a few years perpetrates this example. They tell you to purchase a HELOC (home equity line of credit) through them at 2.5% interest.

They advise you to assign your entire income to their company. You borrow $15,000 from your HELOC and send it to your mortgage payment. They will have calculated out for you how much money you actually need to live on from your paycheck, then you draw against that amount monthly from your HELOC. Yes, you are living on borrowed money.

Now everything else from your paycheck goes to pay down your HELOC balance. When it is paid off, you simply borrow another $15,000 and send it to your mortgage company again, and repeat the process.

A gentleman came to me about a week ago who was so proud that he had embarked upon this brilliant program that is supposed to be prevalent in Australia. He told me how he and his wife assigned, or had their paychecks automatically deposited, into an account that the HELOC company had set up for them. They completely gave up control over their entire paychecks. That amount monthly was $5,800. From that, they needed $3,000 to live on, so they borrowed it from the HELOC. That left $2,800 per month that would go to pay down the HELOC balance.

He told me how he was going to have his $114,000 mortgage paid off in 4.1 years using this method. He almost beamed with pride as he shared this with me. He almost cried, however, when I shared with him that if he did the simple math of applying $2,800 per month under his mattress he would have his house paid off in less than 3 and a half years without earning even one dime of interest. ($114,000 / $2,800 = 40.7months / 12 = 3.39 years)

After doing my research on this program, I learned that he had also sent the HELOC company over $3,900 to set this program up for him, and an additional $1,795 to have online access to his account. While he was doing all this, he still had to make his regular mortgage payments from the $3,000 of borrowed money each month.

Naturally I recommend doing something better with your money than placing it under your mattress, but I think you get the point I'm trying to make here.

Remember, if anyone ever tells you that they have this new and fascinating way to pay your mortgage off early, just like the folks in Australia, run away as fast as you can.

These types of programs are all too accessible, and salesmen make them sound so good. It's time someone told you about these things. I'm thankful to be that person. We have to change the way we view money. We must stop looking for quick fixes, and promises with pie in the sky results.

We must start looking at our personal financial situation independently and systematically. I've heard it said forever that a man who represents himself in court has a fool for a client. Why shouldn't that same idea ring true with our finances? After all, if your attorney is your portal for legal issues, shouldn't you have a professional financial advisor to be your portal to the world of finance?

If you were charged with murder, would you be willing to go to court and gamble the outcome of your future armed only with the advice you received from watching an episode of Perry Mason or Boston Legal, or some other program where entertainers pretend to be attorneys? Then don't gamble your future retirement money on entertainers who pretend to be financial advisors. Oh wait, I think they refer to themselves as financial "Counselors", not advisors.

The difference between working with a financial counselor and a licensed financial advisor is similar to the difference in this example between a volunteer working as a grief counselor and a licensed and experienced clinical psychologist.

The grief counselor is someone you might see after a traumatic situation who gives you a hug and tries to console you by listening to your feelings.

The Clinical Psychologist is someone who will dig deep to find the true cause of your anguish, and work with you over a period of time to help you get through it, and put you on the right track for a productive and fruitful life.

I hope this will help clear up some misconceptions on how much value to place in the advice of some people, and the importance of where you get your information.

Let's take a quick look at a combination of example two and example number three. Those who recommend that you send extra money to the bank to pay your mortgage off early have a good point, and those who recommend you put that extra money into your pre-taxed retirement plan have it partly correct also, but there doesn't seem to be other options that make sense.

I see how sending extra money to the bank certainly accomplishes the one goal of eliminating that mortgage in less time, thereby saving thousands of dollars in interest. What we don't think about is that the bank has already collected the bulk of their interest in the first half of the loan, so the amount saved over the second half of the mortgage will be minimal in comparison.

I also see how obtaining a 15-year mortgage and sending more to your 401(k) can be appealing because of the tax deferred growth of the money taken from your paycheck. What these folks don't tell you is that you will have to pay the IRS back all the money that you deferred in taxes plus interest when you start to withdraw. The money you see in your quarterly statement is not all yours. Part of it belongs to your business partner, the Internal Revenue Service. We'll talk more in detail about this in a later chapter.

Allow me to demonstrate for you a way to pay your home off early, if that's what you want to do when the time comes, retain control of and access to your money all along the way, or to use it for retirement if you so choose, all the while providing for your family in case something happens to you before you are debt free.

This benefit could pass on hundreds of thousands of dollars to your family tax free one day.

Example 4:

I'm sure you have heard people talk about the situations I mentioned just now about ways to build your retirement or pay off your house. Most people look at it like these are the only two options. Here's how each of them work. Feel free to use your calculator to verify what I'm telling you.

Our example is a 35 year old male who doesn't smoke and is in average health. His mortgage amount is $125,000, and all mortgages are assuming a 6% interest rate. The "Buy term insurance and invest the rest" people should read this comparison!

1. Send extra to the bank?

In this scenario, client A decided to obtain a 15-year mortgage so he would have his home paid for by the time he is 50. His monthly mortgage payment is $1,054.82, but he will have accomplished paying his home off in the allotted time. He will have paid the bank his original loan amount plus $64, 867 in interest during that period of time. Client A also would have been advised to purchase a $150,000 life insurance policy to cover his unexpected death. The premiums for that insurance would be on average $21 per month. Total out-of-pocket costs of Client A over fifteen years is $3,660 for life insurance, $125,000 cost of the home, and $64,867 in interest **totaling $193,527**.

In this scenario Client A gives up control over all the money he sends to the bank to pay off his mortgage. If an unexpected illness or loss of employment occurs during the life of the mortgage, he will have to apply to the bank for another loan to access some of the money he has been sending to build equity. Naturally if he has lost his ability to earn an income, he will not qualify for the loan, but he will still have to pay the full $1,054 per month or he will lose his home by foreclosure.

Everyone agrees that you should buy life insurance to cover an unexpected death. Even the entertainers can't argue that point, in fact they encourage it. So why shouldn't we consider using that same insurance while we're alive instead of just in case we die? In the next scenario, I'll show you how to accomplish the same goal, and make sure you can plan for any situation along the way, living or dead.

2. Let the Life Insurance pay off your mortgage, while you're still alive?

Toward the end of this book I'll introduce you to someone who used this type of plan to start a business empire that you will instantly recognize.

Instead of a 15 year, obtain a 30-year mortgage. This will reduce your monthly obligation to the bank, making the monthly mortgage obligation only $750 (saving $304 per month). When you buy the $150,000 life insurance policy, buy universal life instead of term insurance. This will allow you to build a savings fund that will offer financial security literally for a lifetime.

You can buy that permanent insurance policy for as little as $40 per month (minimum premium), but you will want to send in as much as the law will allow. The IRS will allow up to $412 per month on this particular situation without elevated tax consequences. We'll talk in more detail about this later.

Now let's see what will happen if you send just that $325 per month ($304 savings from mortgage plus $21 for term life insurance) to your life insurance vehicle earning 5.2% compound interest (All of these fixed rate policies offer a guaranteed rate of return for the life of the contract), and how quickly you can use it to pay off your home. (Remember that this is the exact amount of money you were already sending to the bank and the insurance company in the other example.)

Using these numbers, you would have enough cash value in your life insurance policy to pay off your mortgage in 16 years. So why would I recommend this strategy over the other? After all, you will have a mortgage for another 12 months, and pay a little more in interest than in the first example. Here's why I believe in this process!

» I believe that people who retain control over, and access to their money will always prevail during challenging economic times.

» How many people lost their homes in the recession of 2008 because of illness or they lost their jobs? How many people would have been able to keep those homes if their monthly obligation was considerably less, like $304 per month maybe?

» How many of those people do you think would have appreciated having access to their money during those difficult times? This type of life insurance allows you complete access to your money when you need it. If you borrow money from your own policy, that money is yours without taxes, or penalties. The death benefit is simply reduced by the amount of the loan when you pass away.

» How many people lost their life insurance during these difficult times? You certainly would not have lost the insurance since your premiums were only about $40 per month. You wouldn't even have to send any money to the insurance company for years in this situation.

» Having a mortgage obligation of $750 per month instead of $1,054 would have allowed you options in the type of job you could get to pay the bills as well. You could flip burgers or accept most any job and be able to keep your family provided with the essentials if your monthly obligations were less. After all, isn't that why you want to pay your house off early in the first place?

» You will still have $159,000 in life insurance that you can never outlive, and the remainder of your cash value which can be added to, if you want to build your retirement fund larger.

» After all, you'll need some kind of an account to put your money in after your mortgage is paid off anyway. It might as well be one that pays you compound interest with tax advantages.

The charts below illustrate how your savings grows to offset your mortgage balance. They also demonstrates the amount you can have access to in case of an emergency without having to borrow from anyone else.

Money you send to the mortgage company and your life

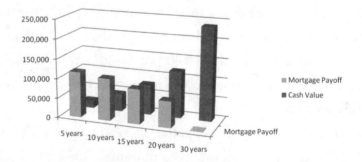

insurance policy each month.

Cash Value Life Insurance vs Mortgage Payoff

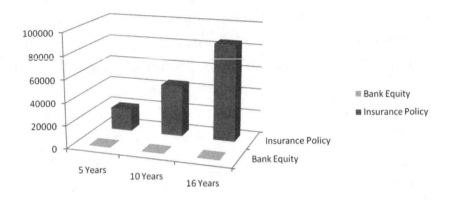

Accessible Cash from the Mortgage Company, or your Life Insurance Policy

You can choose which plan works best for you. I guess you could say I'm a pro-choice financial planner. At least know your choices in how and when you use the money God has entrusted to you.

We've addressed some myths and misunderstandings that people are trying to sell us. Now let's talk about the bigger problem a little bit, and what we're going to do about it.

So many people look at money just like they view food on a buffet line. We want all we can get, as quickly as we can, get it without regard for consequences or risk. With that easy food on the buffet, we are tempted to take more than we actually should, and our waistlines and overall health reflect it.

Then the unseen problems begin to occur, such as obesity, diabetes, and other problems. According to data from The Center for Disease Control and Prevention (cdc.gov) specifically from the National Center for Health Statistics, approximately **66.3% of non-institutionalized adults are overweight or obese**.

Many, after being diagnosed with these health problems, then look for a diet plan that will quickly remedy the situation they caused for themselves over a period of years. They hope to correct the problems in a few days without very much or, preferably no, effort at all. We buy books that sit on the shelf and gather dust. We buy videos because they promise immediate and painless results, and we join a gym only to be discouraged or distracted to the point that we just don't even bother to go back after the first month or two.

I find it interesting that in recent years there has been a similar percentage of Americans who are obese to those suffering from debt-related issues. In drawing a correlation between the buffet, and "easy money," I would like to point out that, just like the "all-you-can eat" buffet, the American banking system has made it increasingly easy for us to borrow all the money we've desired over the past several years.

The handwriting was on the wall years ago; just before 9/11, in their August 27, 2001 issue, *Newsweek* magazine noted that:

"60% of American families actually spend more than their after-tax income, while consumers spend $50 billion more than they earned in April alone. Even more astounding is the fact that 32 million families (i.e. 80 million people) run an annual average deficit of $8,160. These people are exhausting their savings, selling off their investments, and still running huge debts. It will take very little to push them into bankruptcy. For many, just a few months out of work or with reduced income will do the trick."

Similar to the destruction caused by the results of obesity, we find the resulting issues of debt to be people owing more than they can afford to pay back. So many people depend on their current economic situation remaining the same, to the point that if their income dropped even a small percentage they would be unable to meet their obligations.

Another variable that plays a significant role in their ability to meet obligations is the cost factor. This is an element that they cannot control such as gas or food prices. When anything disproportionately increases the amount of capital outlay like gas for the car or food prices, it diminishes the payer's ability to meet their other financial obligations. When we are not living within our means, any fluctuation in money coming in or going out can cause catastrophic financial and emotional results. We then buy finance and "get rich quick" books and videos in hope of a speedy recovery, but end up just throwing even more money away.

We also pay to join financial programs that just like the join a gym idea, we think just by attending, our problems will disappear quickly and painlessly. When we realize there is actual work required on our part, we often fail to finish the program and continue the downward spiral into financial ruin.

The purpose of this book is to provide hope, and help for those people who have found themselves in a challenging financial situation, help them understand what got them there, and offer some assistance in getting out of that overwhelming feeling of hopelessness and despair that comes with such issues.

There is no better place to look for hope than God's word. Remember that Jesus said in **John 15:1-5** *"I am the true vine, and my Father is the gardener. He cuts off every branch that does not produce fruit, and He prunes the branches that do bear fruit so they will produce even more. You have already been pruned for greater fullness by the message I have given with you. Remain in me, and I will remain in you. For a branch cannot produce fruit if it is severed from the vine. And you cannot be fruitful apart from me. Yes, I am the vine; those who remain in me, and I in them will produce much fruit."*

Remember that there is an order which we must address any financial plan, it is:

1. **Active Prayer:** Prayer in which you don't just ask for what you want, but one where you are sincerely seeking God's will in

your life. Spend more time listening to what God tells you, than the time you spend telling Him what you want.

2. **Obey:** When God reveals things to you, obey Him. The only thing that separates those who do great things for His kingdom from those who do not, is the fact that those who did the great things were willing to obey what they heard God reveal to them in focused active prayer.

3. **Tithes and Offerings:** Most people forget that all the money we have belongs to God in the first place. He only asks for 10% back from you for the development of His Kingdom. Offerings, above 10% simply serve to bolster those ministries that focus on spreading His love and witnessing to others. **You can never out give God!**

My prayer is that this book will ENRICH you with knowledge, ENCOURAGE you to open your mind to ideas apart from those given to the masses, and EMPOWER you to accomplish *all* of your financial goals, thereby freeing you up to be a more effective witness for our Father, God. **Romans 8:28** (King James Version) *"And we know that all things work together for good to them that love God, to them who are the called according to his purpose."*

You will find the next chapter encouraging and uplifting. The stories you will read will make you laugh, and put into perspective some issues we all deal with every day. We will also unveil the blueprint of "The Trinity Plan" for you.

Later on I'll give you some real life testimonials from some people who have turned away from the type of advice I've told you about in the earlier examples, and then followed mine, which has changed their lives for the better. I'm proud to not only call these people clients, but also my friends.

Chapter Four

Don't Let Them Get You Down!

For years I have worked directly with families across this country to help them stretch their dollars and understand the best ways to use their money. Time after time I have seen people place their faith in money, and treat it as if it were the only thing in the world that mattered. Several times a day, they watch the stock market to see if they are winning or losing. They will even stop talking about sports long enough to talk about money. The fact that people will interrupt a conversation about their children's baseball or soccer league to discuss finances proves where their focus is.

When was the last time you heard anyone stop talking about sports or money long enough to talk about God? When was the last time you changed the conversation to start talking about how great God is?

There is nothing that will divide a family faster than the relationship with their money. With the divorce rate in America exceeding 50%, we have to get a handle on this destructive issue. In 2007 I was asked by Donald E. Wildmon, the founder of The American Family Association, what I thought was the number one issue American Families were dealing with at the time. My reply was immediate: finances.

It doesn't matter if they don't have enough money to pay the bills, or they have an abundance of it, money divides more families than even infidelity. People who fall short of their budget month in and month out often develop resentment toward one another. Sometimes they feel their spouse either has spent too much on something they could have done without, or they feel like the other one could do more to bring additional funds into the home. Of course they never talk about their feelings toward that issue. This causes the pressure to build up like steam in a pressure cooker. If you allow it to build and build it could explode and be devastating to the relationship.

These folks didn't intentionally allow this divide to occur, but they didn't intentionally do anything to avoid it either. That's where we come in. When you understand what the problem is, you can take steps to begin closing that divide. This will allow you to reduce the building pressure in your relationship through finances.

To protect your family, you need to be careful where you receive your information, how you implement that information, and the habits you form through that implementation. Do you get your advice from those who are enriching you with the knowledge you need to achieve your goals? Are you receiving information from people who are encouraging you to reach beyond what is accepted as "the norm," or are you hearing them tell you that "You can't do that" because it isn't what everyone else is doing?

The old adage "misery loves company" comes to mind when I think about people who take advice from their peers who are walking down the wide path of this world. Now is the time to do something different than what is accepted as "the norm." If you want to begin receiving better than normal results, you must begin doing things that aren't considered normal by the masses.

I heard a story some time ago about three gorillas placed in a large cage at a zoo. The zoo keepers were conducting a behavioral experiment to see what the animals would do when discouraged from an otherwise normal behavioral trait, such as obtaining their food of choice, bananas. The three gorillas, who didn't know one another before they were placed together, came from a variety of backgrounds. But as they entered the cage, they each immediately noticed that there was a rope hanging from the ceiling in the middle of the room, and a large bunch of bananas hanging next to it.

> "A man can live 40 days without food, four days without water, four minutes without air, but only four seconds without hope."
> —Rev. Dr. John C. Maxwell

They all made their way to the rope, but were immediately drenched with several fire hoses as they reached for the delectable treat. They were driven back and forced to formulate another plan. After a little while, they all tried again to reach the bananas, but once again they were driven back by the fire hoses.

This went on for some time until finally they just gave up. Every time they tried to do something for themselves, they were discouraged until they just realized there was no hope in ever achieving their goal, so they just stopped trying. (Sound familiar to anyone?)

After about two weeks, one of the original gorillas was removed from the cage, and a new gorilla was introduced to the others.

The new gorilla thought he had entered the perfect place when he saw the huge bunch of bananas hanging from the center of the room. As he made his way to the rope, however, he was instantly tackled by the other two gorillas. Every time he went for the fruit, the other two, remembering the fire hoses, tackled him to avoid the deluge of cold water.

This went on for some time, until the new gorilla finally just gave up on ever trying to obtain his much desired reward. After another week, the second of the original three gorillas was removed and replaced with another gorilla that also had not experienced the blasts of cold water. Just like the earlier arrival, the new gorilla tried to climb the rope to the fresh bananas that were just hanging there for his enjoyment. Before he could begin climbing the rope to his ultimate reward, the other two grabbed him and pulled him to the ground. Once again this activity was repeated until the new roommate just stopped trying. About a week passed again until the last of the three original gorillas was removed from the cage. He was replaced with another new gorilla who had never witnessed the fire hoses at work.

Now none of the current gorillas had ever seen or experienced the rush of cold water from the fire hoses as a deterrent from their activity to grab a banana from the center of the room. Even though the other two gorillas had not experienced the deluge, as the new animal ran toward the rope to ascend to the fresh bunch of delicious bananas, they grabbed him and wrestled him to the floor. Once again this activity continued until none of the three gorillas, even though they had never experienced the negative event, just didn't even try to reach their desired goals.

Have you ever had someone try to keep you down without really understanding why? Now is the time to develop a plan to reach your bananas. What goals do you have that you didn't think you could actually achieve because others told you it wasn't possible?

Break away from the primates, and seek out the advice of professionals who will help you accomplish your goals. Don't get into your elderly years and start asking yourself *What if I had just tried one more time?*

In the absence of a complete plan and encouragement to stick with it, we can all too often be swayed to believe what some others would have us believe. As Christians, we cannot accept that exposure to incorrect information and guidance. When you have a solid plan in place and a good understanding of why it is there, and experienced Christian counselors trained to offer timely advice built around a solid foundational principle, you shouldn't be able to be swayed too much. Let's face it, we all make mistakes, but we are less likely to make catastrophic mistakes when we are well grounded in belief and principle, and accountable to Christian brothers and sisters.

This gorilla story is a perfect example of how we have been trained by the teachings of (I would like to believe) well intending organizations and individuals and become distracted from reaching our goals. They tell us to depend on what they give us and don't even look for other ways to accomplish our desired results. Have you ever been so discouraged or even knocked down when you've tried to accomplish something on your own, because the way you wanted to go about it wasn't what someone else said was "the right way"? I dare say many of us have.

But as Christians, we understand that often times, God allows us to undergo challenges, and even failures, to strengthen our commitment to Him. As His witnesses, He needs us to undergo such trials so we can help our brothers and sisters when we see them going through similar events. It's hard to understand where someone is in their walk if you haven't been there yourself.

What makes me uniquely qualified to bring this message to you is because I have been to the top of the financial mountain and seen the incredible life that can await us. I have also been to the pit of despair, having lost my family in divorce, my job because of adultery, my home because of poor planning, and my hope because of not knowing where to turn.

Years ago, while God was taking away all the things that I had placed in an order of importance above Him, I didn't understand that none of those worldly things really mattered if my soul was destined to spend eternity in Hell. God is still working in my life every day to teach and encourage me to be the best witness for Him that I can be. I hope that this book will serve as a tool to show you that there is hope for your situation, no matter what you might understand from those with the hoses who are aiming to discourage you at every turn.

God wants others to follow you when you are living a life pleasing to Him. He will give you all the resources you need to attract these followers, including financial prosperity. If you have issues that prevent you from being that person who would attract others to follow you into a relationship with Christ, you must re-focus so you can be that beacon that others need to see, and guide them into that special knowledge of salvation that we enjoy and hold dear.

God wants you to enjoy life in abundance and realize all the blessings that He has in store for those who turn their focus from "the world" and place it instead on serving Him. As we unveil the Trinity Plan, you will be better able to understand how God has prepared you for exactly where you are right now, but more importantly, where He wants you to go from here.

In order to better understand how this plan works, you must first see that there are three major issues relating to finance. The first issue is effective **money management**. The second is developing a better understanding of how you **save money wisely**. The third issue relating to finances is how to **protect the assets** you have worked so diligently for your entire working life. You will become a much better steward of God's gifts when you understand all three of these important financial topics.

Now let's go to the next chapter where I will begin to reveal the Trinity Plan to you.

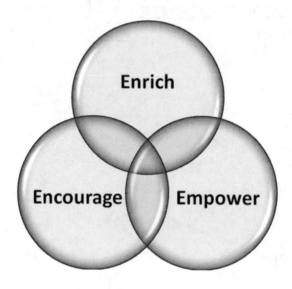

The Trinity Plan

Chapter Five

"The Trinity Plan" A Three Step Process to Prosperity

W hen I started in this business, most people still believed that only the wealthiest people in our country had money in the stock market and that "common folks" like you and I had to follow their trends and ideas. Typically, those passing along investing information were the same ones profiting from our actions, or inactions. I guess this philosophy really hasn't changed all that much.

For the past several years, God has allowed me to see information little bits at a time, until He finally revealed the entire "Trinity Plan" to me. He would give me pieces of the plan that made perfect sense, but these pieces weren't always what commentators on television or radio were talking about as the "right thing" to do with money. As time went on, I shared this information with co-workers and clients. People were thankful to have truth, and a sensible plan that they could use to safely build wealth. They also realized that, just as my grandfather said, "Rome wasn't built in a day".

We all understand that patience is rewarded in the long term, but that's often hard to understand in the beginning. You can understand this when you recall what Albert Einstein said was the most incredible thing he had ever witnessed. "The most powerful force in the universe is compound interest," he said. Of all the bright and ingenious ideas Mr. Einstein discovered and witnessed, compound interest was the most amazing to him. If this idea was good to one of the brightest men in history, why don't we take advantage of this phenomenon today? Because we want everything right away!

That's what happened when Moses was leading the people of Israel out of captivity from Egypt. Driven by greed, they were impatient and often turned from God, and worshipped their own idols in the hope of receiving instant gratification. Their failure to obey and disregard for God caused them to never see "The Promised Land." Our own greed, disobedience, and disregard for God's will may be the underlying issue that explains why we experience financial difficulties in the first place. We actually turn to our money as "our God." I say this because, if you spend more time thinking about, talking about, or dealing with anything other than God, then that idol has replaced Him as your focus.

In an effort to help re-focus people, I developed The Trinity Plan, which came about by asking, What would a great and complete financial program look like? When I saw that there were already so many books written on the subject of finance and money by economists and others who treat everyone's unique individual needs the same way, I realized that I needed to develop a program that wasn't a "one-size-fits-all" approach. I also needed to understand that the money we are talking about isn't ours to begin with, but God's, and that He has given us responsibility to ensure its wise use until He asks for an accounting one day.

As I developed The Trinity Plan, the word "**complete**" kept surfacing, so I turned to the Bible for answers. The plan that was developing in my mind kept emphasizing the importance of the number three. I consulted with people far more knowledgeable about the scriptures than myself.

I was overwhelmed to learn that three is the number that signifies completion in God's word. When I learned the significance of the number, it was only natural to call this plan for God's people "The Trinity Plan". It seemed as though God had placed the capstone on His program.

I realized that any complete plan must include a method of distributing general information to people in an effort to enrich them with knowledge. It had to be one that instilled confidence to encourage people to step out of their comfort zone and venture out on faith.

"If you want happiness for an hour — take a nap. If you want happiness for a day — go fishing. If you want happiness for a month — get married. If you want happiness for a year — inherit a fortune. If you want happiness for a lifetime — help someone else."

It had to also empower them to take action with guidance from a Christian financial professional who would serve, in accordance with **Proverbs 15:22**, as a wise counselor to be a constant resource for the family.

Accordingly, the three major components of **The Trinity Plan** are:

>> **Enrich** people with knowledge

>> **Encourage** people with confidence

>> **Empower** them to step away from a worldly view, with constant support from trusted Christian professionals.

Through public events, we begin enriching people with general information. Then, through a free one-on-one consultation with a "Certified Money Coach" (this designation is not a professional designation, just certifies the financial professional meets all criteria to be a member of our team), a licensed and experienced Christian financial professional, they are provided with encouraging words of hope.

After all necessary information has been gathered, the team of "Money Coaches" can develop a plan specifically for that family, which will empower them to take the recommended actions to begin seeing positive results. Finally, clients have a private meeting with all the specialists needed to implement their strategy, based on the goals stated during their initial consultation. Over the coming years, however, the money coach remains as a constant resource for the family, monitoring the success of the plan and making make necessary adjustments as life changes occur.

According to **Luke 16:13** (Life Application Study Bible), Jesus said, *"No one can serve two masters. For you will hate the one and love the other, or you will be devoted to one and despise the other. You cannot serve both God and money"*. Before you can begin your journey to an abundant life, you must first understand that money, in and of itself, is never the underlying problem in any situation. "It's how we view it, use it, and worship it that allows money to become a tool with which we cultivate the true underlying issue(s)".

All too often these underlying issues or seeds that we cultivate with that money are greed, envy, pride, vanity, anger, jealousy, or selfishness.

I can place a $1 bill, a $10 bill, and a $100 bill on a table and leave them there for 100 years, and they will never argue or fight among themselves, cause war, divorce, or plot harm against one another. Not until humans lust after the money, contemplate all the different ways they can use it, or spend it on ungodly things does the money ever become harmful to a spiritual life. If you aren't sure about what I'm saying, ask yourself some hard questions.

1. Why do I have a car payment? Couldn't I have bought a less expensive vehicle that would get me to where I need to go, or do I just feel the need to show myself off in the nicest and newest car or truck I can borrow the money to get? **Is this a vanity thing?** Was this a want or a need?

2. Why did I lose so much money in the stock market? Couldn't I have found smarter ways to save my money? Was I just looking for a fast, easy way to turn a little bit of money into a lot of money? Did I lose control over my money because I was willing to gamble that it would multiply itself? **Is this a greed thing?** Was this a want or a need?

3. Why did I go out and buy that new computer on credit after my spouse asked me not to? Was I just looking for a way to get back at them for a situation I wasn't happy about? Could I have saved some money and eventually paid for it in cash? **Is this an anger thing?** Was this a want or a need?

All of these situations are actual issues that some of my clients have discussed with me, as we worked to get them out from under a world of debt. As I said, the money didn't cause any of these problems; it was how the money was used that caused these difficulties.

I am very blessed to have the opportunities to speak all over this great country and meet some wonderful people who just need a little guidance in regard to their finances. When speaking to groups, I always ask people two questions.

The first question is: What is a national park or monument they would like to visit before they die? Without fail there are always some of the same places that are shouted back from the crowd: The Grand Canyon, Mount Rushmore, Yosemite National Park, and Niagara Falls.

The reason I do this is to drive home the point that if you know where you are starting from, and exactly where you are going, you can plan the best route to take that will get you there. The reason we always hear these same places is that people can visualize them in their minds, because they have seen pictures, videos or magazine articles describing them explicitly. When you can actually see where you want to be, it becomes more achievable and real to you.

The second question is: What does financial freedom mean to you? This obviously conjures up a multitude of thoughts, and even anxiety for some. After a moment or so, I take people off the hook and display slides that demonstrate what financial freedom is to some people. For some, financial freedom is having $50 dollars left over at the end of the month with no one calling or writing them to get it. For others, it's having enough money left over to take the family out to eat at a restaurant without a drive thru window once in a while. Many would like to have a savings account with enough money in it to replace the refrigerator if it went out. Then there are always those who consider having $250,000 or more in a retirement account to be financial freedom.

I never get quick responses to this question, because everyone is different. It's also a very abstract question, because we don't see pictures, videos or magazine articles that help us visualize exactly what financial freedom is specifically for us.

This is the part of the presentation where I find one of the smallest people in the room and ask them to come forward. I always invite my wife to join me if she is in attendance. She is only five feet tall, and very petite. I take my jacket off, and place it on her. Keep in mind that I am 6 feet 6 inches tall, and am a rather large man. Since the person coming forward is always much smaller than myself, my coat always swallows them.

This is the way I help people visualize why we buy different sized clothes for ourselves, and we're very careful to make sure things fit before we pay for them. People have different tastes in food, clothes, the type of house they live in, and the car they drive.

If we wouldn't spend $10 for a t-shirt that doesn't fit, even though it says "one-size-fits-all", why would we allow our entire financial future to fall prey to such a sales technique?

I love what God's word says in **Matthew 7:13-14** about following the crowd. (New King James Version) *"Enter by the narrow gate; for wide is the gate and broad is the way that leads to destruction, and there are many who go in by it. Because narrow is the gate and difficult is the way which leads to life, and there are few who find it.*

When we follow the ones who are also seeking the narrow path to eternal life, we are doing what is pleasing to God. Stop following the masses on the wide path, and walk with God's people on the narrow path. There are fewer of us, but we know where our path leads.

"But, dear friends, remember what the apostles of our Lord Jesus Christ foretold. They said to you, "In the last times there will be scoffers who will follow their own ungodly desires."
Jude 17–18
—NIV

I have heard myths for years and years about how to get rich quick, or how to make money fast. These so called plans are of the world, not of God. In **1ˢᵗ John 2:15** (Life Application Study Bible), The Bible says, *"Do not love the world, nor the things in the world. If anyone loves the world, the love of the Father is not in him. For all that is in the world, the lust of flesh and the lust of the eyes and the boastful pride of life, is not from the Father, but is of the world"*. Let's take a look at why we, as Christians have to look beyond the false teachings of this world.

We'll begin addressing specific financial issues in the next chapter that will offer a clear understanding of some changes that might need to be explored in your particular situation.

Chapter Six

"Money Management"

$

U nfortunately, when we discuss "money management" today, we are most likely talking about debt management. Because of greed, envy, pride, vanity, anger, jealousy, selfishness, and the need to have everything "RIGHT NOW", people have lost the understanding of the old adage, "If you don't have the cash, don't buy it".

It seems as though young people in particularly believe that they should immediately be able to go out and buy a house just as big, or bigger, than their parents right after getting their first job. They look at what their parents worked a lifetime to have and feel entitled to live just as well. Financial institutions support this thought with seemingly never ending offers for credit, and the picture of having the "American Dream" right away. They cause us to believe that everyone is doing it, and we would be crazy not to follow the same path everyone else is enjoying.

One thing I have noticed over the years is that there seems to be two types of people: those who work hard for their money, and those who let money work hard for them. Those who work hard for their money just get tired. Those who let money work hard for them get wealthy.

Which one of these pictures do you more closely associate with your financial situation?

If you're like most people, you will associate more closely with the young lady trying to wake up and start another day at the same old grindstone. If that is the case, you need to listen to the definition I love of insanity. I've heard it defined as this "doing the same thing over and over, expecting a different result".

You will never change the results until you begin changing the habits that got you to where you are. You cannot change those habits until you analyze why you did the things that you did that brought you here. And you can never identify those issues until you are honest about them, and confide in someone you can openly speak with in Christian love.

Time after time I have met with couples who clean the slate between them so they can move forward, not only in their finances but also their relationship. So often one of them, husband or wife, has been holding back feelings or information that has caused friction between them. Often they blame these things on their money problems, or they use money to get back at one another. Money Coaches are there to assist that Christian brother or sister open the lines of communication that are so vital to the success of any relationship.

We have been tracking the spending habits of people we have worked with for several years now, and have designed a graph that accurately demonstrates where people's money goes. Every new client is given an asset allocation form that is completed before we ever work with them. From these forms, we have gathered statistical data which is demonstrated for you in the following graph.

When we look at the typical new client we find that the chart below offers a pretty good distribution of their current assets We find that approximately 30% of their income is going to pay for their mortgage, 15% is paying for their car payment(s) 11% is being sent to credit card

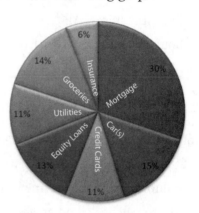

companies, 13% goes back to the bank for an equity loan, 11% to utilities such as electric, gas, phone etc., 14% goes to groceries, and 6% is being paid to insurance companies. As Christians, we must look at these numbers and ask, What's missing from this chart?

There are three obvious things that are missing:

1. Tithes and offerings
2. Personal Savings
3. Emergency Fund

This is what we usually see to be true:

1. **Tithes and offerings** / We give from what's left over at the end of the pay cycle
2. **Personal Savings** / This is almost always the 401(k) plan at work
3. **Emergency Fund** / Inevitably, the family's credit cards

I find it easier to understand strategies and concepts when I understand the meaning of words related to those strategies and concepts. In keeping with that thought, I would like to offer to you a definition of debt that I have found to be fairly accurate over the years, both in my own life as well in the lives of those with whom I've worked. I've found that debt is a convenient way to borrow money to acquire typically non-essential items All too often we see new furniture in homes that was bought with a credit card, or vacations to places like Disney World where, instead of saving the money before they go, the family charges the whole trip and pays for it over a period of several years.

Of course they also pay back a larger amount in interest than they probably would have earned if they had saved the money in advance. An $8,000 vacation charged on a credit card at 16% interest will result in a minimum monthly payment of $320 that will take 12 years and 11 months to pay back, and an additional $4,111.03 in interest, making the grand total paid for that week-long vacation $12,111.03 – 50% more than they actually thought they were spending.

This is a perfect illustration of what I always say: People who understand interest earn it, while those who do not understand pay it. Banks and other lending institutions make trillions of dollars based on that one fact alone.

But, you ask, what about the wealthy people who build hotels, restaurants, and housing developments? You can't believe that they pay cash for everything! You're exactly correct in that assumption. When wealthy people use money to accomplish the missions that you just described they use a term called leverage.

My definition of leveraging is quite the opposite of debt. Leverage is an effective way to use other people's money to accomplish strategic financial goals. Have you heard of the phrase called O.P.M. (other people's money) in regards to how people with money make more money? This practice is exactly how banks and other lending institutions make money off of your money. I love teaching people how to begin doing that for themselves.

If you have that $8,000 in credit at 16% interest, and need a way to pay it off in a much shorter time than the almost 13 years earlier described, you can simply apply an additional $25 per month to the payment and wipe out that balance in two years and five months, and save $2,439 in interest. Imagine what would happen if you could send more than $25. So many of the people we currently meet with don't have the additional $25 per month, lending even more credibility to the fact that if you don't have the money, you shouldn't spend it.

LIVE WITHIN YOUR MEANS! Many people today believe that is a cruel phrase, and say that we are trying to withhold the good life from people without money. Do I even need to say anything about that? The illustration below shows you how you can live within your means. Assume you have two credit cards totaling $8,000 at a blended interest rate of 16%.

Debt Elimination Plan (The Avalanche Method)

I call this the Avalanche method because it causes the whole banking world to crumble around them when you figure out how to beat them at their own game. The Avalanche method could help you save **$2,439** in interest charges, or even more if you apply it effectively.

You owe a total of **$8,000**. Your current minimum monthly payment is **$320**. **If you continue to make the minimum payments the total interest paid will be $4,111.** It will take you **12 years and 11 months** to payoff this debt. Using the credit card Avalanche method your total payments would be **$345**, which includes an **additional $25 per month**. The Avalanche method could help you pay **$2,439 less** in interest. In addition, the time it will take you to pay off your credit cards is reduced to **two years and five months**. This analysis assumes that each month you apply your Avalanche amount to **pay off your highest interest rate first**.

Avalanche Debt Summary

	Amount Owed	Interest Rate	Monthly Payment
Credit card 1	$5,000	18.90%	$200
Credit card 2	$3,000	12.00%	$120
Total	$8,000	16.31%	$320

Avalanche Payment Schedule

	Current Payment Schedule			Avalanche Payment Schedule		
Year	Payments	Interest	Balance	Payments	Interest	Balance
			$8,000			$8,000
1	$3,329	$1,135	$5,806	$4,140	$1,083	$4,943
2	$2,417	$830	$4,218	$4,140	$543	$1,347
3	$1,757	$607	$3,068	$1,392	$46	$0
4	$1,279	$445	$2,234	$0	$0	$0
5	$932	$326	$1,629	$0	$0	$0
6	$679	$239	$1,188	$0	$0	$0

7	$497	$176	$868	$0	$0	$0
8	$388	$128	$608	$0	$0	$0
9	$319	$89	$377	$0	$0	$0
10	$173	$59	$263	$0	$0	$0
11	$121	$43	$185	$0	$0	$0
12	$120	$27	$92	$0	$0	$0
13	$101	$8	$0	$0	$0	$0

We've mentioned credit cards; now let's take a look at your mortgage. Let's say you borrowed $125,000 to purchase your home at 6% interest over 30 years. Assuming no refinancing, you will have paid back to the bank or other lending institution a total of $265,000. That includes your original loan amount of $125,000 plus $140,000 in interest paid over 30 years. Today so many "experts" tell you to send extra money to the bank to pay down the balance of your mortgage.

The reasoning behind that is sound enough, but let me ask you, what happens if you need some of that money that you have sent to the bank as extra payments? If you are out of work, or need to make some repairs to your home, how will you be able to access your money? That's right, you have to complete loan papers, and ask the bank if you can borrow some of your own money. If you don't have a job, or are having financial problems that would inhibit your ability to repay the loan, the bank will not give your money back to you in the first place. Even though the basic concept sounds prudent, the actual real life scenario isn't such a good thing for most people.

My advice is to set up an account in either an investment grade fixed interest life insurance policy with a guaranteed minimum interest rate or a fixed rate annuity or Roth IRA. Then send your extra money to your own account and let it earn compound interest for you.

Albert Einstein

Remember what Albert Einstein said about the power of compound interest. The reason I choose these types of accounts is that they are typically protected by law; if you are sued for any reason, the lawyers (in most States) cannot access these funds. They can take away your mutual funds, savings accounts, money market accounts, checking accounts and even the equity in your home, but creditors cannot seize money in and death benefit of annuities and life insurance in most states. By holding a 30-year mortgage for $125,000 for 30 years, your monthly payments will be $749.44 (not including taxes or insurance), and in 10 years, you will still have $104,380.75 left to pay on your loan. But if you paid the bank $200 extra every month, your pay off in 10 years is only $71,241.01. Pretty good deal, wouldn't you say?

I see why so many people recommend this strategy, but let's look at it another way. What if, instead of sending that same $200 to the bank you use it to earn something for yourself? In 10 years, your mortgage payoff will still be $104, 380, but the equity you invested in your new savings instrument paying 5% interest has grown to $31,186 that you control. Subtracting the $31,186 from your payoff of $104,380 makes your actual payoff $73,194. And that's only $1,953 more than the payoff you would have owed if you gave the bank holding your mortgage control of all your money.

How much it is worth to retain control over the money you work so hard for? I'd say it's worth at least $1,953. You see, everything that's sold to the masses is not always in our best interest. And if it's not in our best interest, it's not in God's best interest either.

I hope the next chart will give you a clear understanding of how the flow of your money works when you decide to send extra money to the bank to pay your mortgage off early. The alternate option in the second chart may cause you to rethink everything you've been told by banks about the best way to pay your home off early.

"Typical Structure of Your Mortgage Payments"

In this structure, you must apply to the bank to apply for access to your equity, because they hold control over all the money you sent to them in your effort to pay your home off faster. In order to access your equity, you must complete loan papers and then wait for a decision about whether or not the bank will loan you back your own money.

Now let's take a look at another option, and you decide which one gives you better access to your money, and thus, better control over how and when it will be used.

"Alternate Option for Paying Off Your Mortgage Early"

This graph demonstrates that you can still build equity on your home by paying your regular mortgage payment, but you use any extra money to build additional equity, in an account that you control and have access to when you need it, or decide to use it, perhaps to pay your home off in less than 30 years. The chart below (Table 1) demonstrates how $200 extra per month on a $125,000 30-year, fixed rate mortgage financed at 6% can reduce the amount of time you have to pay on it significantly.

In this scenario you can have your mortgage paid off in just over 18 years by either sending the extra money to the bank or sending it to an account you control. In one, you have access to your money; in the other, the bank controls all your equity and can deny you access to it unless you qualify for a new loan. If you lose your job you won't qualify for the loan, and if your financial situation is difficult you may not qualify either.

Both are reasons you might need access to your money in the first place, right? So let's see, you can achieve the same results either way, but retain control over my money one way, or completely lose control the other way. This should be a no brainer. (See Table 1 for this example)

Table 1

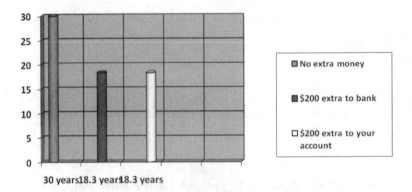

Another thought to keep in mind is the amount of money you actually have access to, without borrowing or incurring tax implications if you have an emergency, such as the loss of your job, or an illness in the family, or if you just want to pay off all your debt. The chart below demonstrates all the money you will be able to access in the same scenarios listed above. (See Table 2 for chart)

Table 2

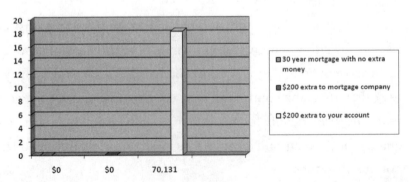

If you are interested in more information about any of these strategies or concepts, you can contact The Abundant Life Institute at www.godsdollar.com. One of our certified money coaches will contact you, and give you information that will *enrich* your life with knowledge, *encourage* you to try something different from the masses, and *empower* you to begin getting better results for God's money. Once you contact a money coach or attend one of our "Abundant Life" workshops, you will learn the three phases of money management that will get you on your way to building wealth. The three steps are:

1. Understand where you are financially, and how you got there.
2. Set clear and achievable goals, and write them down.
3. Work with a certified Money Coach to help you reach all your financial goals.

In regard to setting clear and achievable goals, I remember a story I heard about a research project conducted the Harvard Business School. Story has it that in 1979 they encouraged 20 of their top students to set goals for 10 years. They had 10 of their MBA students write down their goals, and 10 verbally state their goals, but not write them down. In 1989, these same students came back to class to find out how many of them had achieved their goals.

Of the 10 who had written them down, eight had accomplished all their goals. Of the 10 who had not written them down, only two had accomplished their desired results. This study supports the fact that writing down your goals enhances your ability to accomplish those goals, along with ability and opportunity. This is why we ask all our clients to write down exactly what they want us to help them accomplish. You can never get to the Grand Canyon if you're not sure where you're starting from, or if you're not sure where you're going. Financial independence is exactly the same way.

Example of an effective way to manage the use of your assets:

John and Sarah are 32 years old with three children. Their youngest child is eight weeks old and Sarah is faced with having to go back to her full time job. She really wants to stay home and be a full time wife and mother. This would reduce their household income by $1,500 per month.

If they did not have credit card debt of $8,278, which requires a payment of $408 a month, Sarah would be able to stay home. Jon makes enough money to continue their current lifestyle without Sarah's paycheck. Other than the debt and mortgage payment, their household expenses are only $1,384. John makes $72,000 per year, and health insurance for the family is taken out of his paycheck, but he has no life insurance. He brings home $3,946 per month.

They bought their home six years ago for $125,000, and pay $749 per month. They have one car valued at $8,350 that they owe $10,324 on, and are paying $528 per month. Money is tight, but they are dedicated to making this change for the good of their family. How can we at The Abundant Life Institute help them make this happen?

Here's the recommendation for this case.

Original Monthly Situation:

- » $749 paid to mortgage
- » $0 toward savings
- » $0 life insurance
- » $400 paid to Credit Cards
- » $528 paid to Car payment
- » Mortgage paid off in 24 years.

New Monthly Strategy
- » $659 to mortgage
- » $1,000 toward savings
- » $425,000+ in life insurance
- » $0 paid to credit cards
- » $0 to car payments
- » Mortgage paid off in 7 years, if desired

Much more data was collected and analyzed in this actual situation, but for your convenience I am summarizing this strategy:

The current appraised value of their home is $149,500. I recommended that they refinance their current 8%, 30-year, fixed rate mortgage, and put their equity to work for them. The new loan reduces their monthly mortgage payment by $90 per month. Through strategic alliances with a mortgage broker, I know we can obtain a lower interest rate than what they currently have. In this example, the mortgage company can provide a 5.28% rate amortized over 30 years. They refinanced for a new loan amount of $119,600 (accessing 80% of their total equity), paid off the remaining balance of $96,501 on their existing loan, and received $21,299 in cash at closing, after total closing costs of $1,800 were paid.

With that money, they paid off the credit cards. They're no longer sending the credit card company 17% in interest, and the bank 8% on their mortgage. They've freed up an amazing $1,018 per month that they had been sending to creditors. I recommended that this family redirect this monthly savings into a savings tool that can generate compound interest for them, be safe from any potential creditors, and give them access to their money if needed.

Result:

They took the full amount that they had been sending in monthly payments to the credit card company and the bank, and started putting this money into investment-grade life insurance on John. He wisely chose to send the full $1,018 per month to a cash-value life insurance instrument.

Allow me to briefly explain why this particular financial vehicle is right for this situation. John needs life insurance, but doesn't know exactly when he will die, so he chooses to use a type of coverage that will make him money while he is still living, and not simply another monthly bill like term life insurance.

To put it simply, the differences between permanent life insurance and term life insurance is like the difference between buying a home and renting a house. In one you build equity and know you will always be covered. With the other you do not build equity, and have nothing to show for the money you spent at the end of the term.

John chose permanent life insurance also because it typically pays much higher rate of return that a savings account at your bank, grows tax deferred, and is accessible cash if he needs it for anything. Plus he knows that the death benefit portion of this type of coverage will always be there to protect his family, even when he can't.

Using this tool will give them the flexibility to reduce contributions should any unexpected event occur, and increase contributions if they receive extra money.

In seven years, John will owe only $84,484 on his mortgage, but will have enough cash value ($92,656) to write a check and pay his house off if he chooses, saving $26,429 in interest. Or he can choose to keep paying his mortgage, which is a tax deduction for his family, and keep growing the money he once had sent to creditors. If he continued on this plan, by the time he reaches 65, the cash value in his policy will be worth $856,159, and he can use the money as a retirement account.

Either way, John and his family win because they regain, and maintain control over their money which gives them choices. They also have access to this cash in case they need to replace their car, or use some of the money for other costs that require a little extra cash. I didn't even mention the secure feeling that John now has because he has provided for his family in the event of his unexpected death. He began the program with $425,000 of death benefit.

With the expert assistance of their money coach they can now realize financial independence. This means they are essentially debt free after seven years. They can then choose to let their money continue to grow, retain access to and control over all their money, and no longer ever have to worry about asking anyone else for a loan again.

These goals were accomplished because the family wrote their goals down and shared them with a Christian professional who guided them through the process, and regularly monitored their progress. The family was committed to seeing different results, and had the confidence to reject a "one-size-fits-all" message. Now, if God called for an accounting of His gifts, they could definitely give a good report that would earn the reply from Him, "Well done, my good and faithful servant." Which plan would you rather have? (See table 3)

Table 3

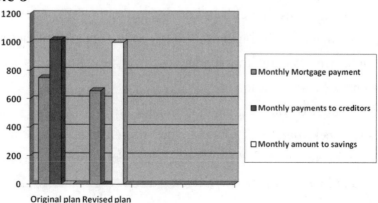

I hope this real life example gives you a better understanding of the difference between the destructive power of debt and the positive power of effective leveraging. Which way do you want to live? Sending your hard-earned money to others so they can profit from it, or use it effectively so that *you* can profit from it? Please do not attempt this without professional guidance. Our money coaches will help you for free, but your situation may be different from the one illustrated, and remember, this is not a one-size-fits-all program! If used incorrectly, this information can even do more harm than good.

I have obtained some information that might be helpful to some people who have already caused some credit difficulties for themselves. There is also helpful information for those who want to check their credit report, but do not know where to go for that help, and for you who have checked their report and found errors. The articles below will give you helpful tips for correcting credit issues of all kinds. The following information came from interest.com, and was written by editors of that website.

Improving Your Credit Score

Obtaining and Understanding Your Credit Report

Whether you get that credit card may depend on a network of credit reporting agencies that either share information with, or are owned by, three major credit bureaus. Credit reports are critical factors in credit scoring systems that lenders use to issue credit cards, as well as mortgages or other loans.

So, if you're considering making a major financial move, it's a good idea to check your credit report to know where you stand. That way you can be aware of, and if necessary take care of, problems before they derail your plans.

If you find problems, or if potential creditors discover them, take steps to rebuild damaged credit and clean up that record.

If you've made mistakes in paying previous loans, bounced checks, made late payments or had other problems, you may still be able to reduce the amount of damage they will do to your credit with explanations or some basic repair.

Getting your credit report Obtaining copies of your credit reports is easy. The 2003 Fair and Accurate Credit Transactions Act guarantees everyone **one free credit report** from each of the main credit reporting agencies — Equifax, Experian and TransUnion — per year.

You must request your free credit reports through a centralized source. To order online, visit *annualcreditreport.com*. By phone, call (877) 322-8228. Or you may complete the form on the back of the Annual Credit Report Request brochure and mail it to: *Annual Credit Report Request Service, P.O. Box 105283, Atlanta, GA, 30348-5283.*

Two more ways to receive a free copy of your credit report:

» If you applied for a loan and were turned down, you can request a copy by writing the correct credit bureau within 60 days of the rejection. With your request, you should include a copy of the declined loan application.

» You can also get a free report if you are unemployed, planning to apply for a job in the next 60 days, receiving public welfare assistance or believe the credit file contains mistakes resulting from fraud.

If you wish to purchase your credit report (beyond your free copies) ... request a copy from each of the three credit bureaus: Equifax, Experian and TransUnion.

Time it, then check the details If you are about to apply for a major loan such as a house or car, it's important to give yourself time to correct mistakes or make good on delinquent accounts.

To give yourself enough time, here's a guideline:

» For a home, you should check your credit at least three to six months before you apply for a mortgage.

» For an auto loan, check your credit (and arrange financing with your bank or credit union) before you start shopping.

» For credit cards, check your report before you apply. The last thing you need is for a credit report problem to slow down your application -- particularly if it's not your fault.

Once you get the report, you should make sure the following information is correct.

Double-check the following:

» Your name or names, if you are or were married

» Social Security number

» Date of birth

» Addresses of places you've lived

» Names of places you've worked

» Pending accounts and accounts that have been closed

» Records of delinquent payments or other problems (i.e., make sure they're not mistakes)

Next, make sure nothing has been on the report longer than is allowed by law.

Used-by dates:

» Bankruptcies must be taken off your credit history after 10 years

» Suits, judgments, tax liens and most other kinds of unfavorable financial information must be dropped after seven years. If unpaid, tax liens can remain on the report for up to 15 years.

Get all of them "Looking at one is a useless endeavor; you need to look at all three," says Howard Dvorkin, president of Consolidated Credit Counseling Services in Fort Lauderdale, Fla. "People tend to pull one and think everything is the same on all of them. That's not normally the case."

The reports will have different information because it's a voluntary system, and creditors subscribe to whichever agency they want -- if any at all.

Maxine Sweet, vice president of public education at Experian, stresses the importance of ordering the report directly from the credit bureau instead of asking a buddy who works at a bank to pull one for you. Those are written for people who work in the credit industry. The one you get from the credit bureau is designed for consumers.

"The information is the same, but it's much more consumer-friendly," she says.

Well, not quite the same. But the differences, Sweet says, are only to make the report easier for consumers to read. The report sent to a lender will list the credit bureau member numbers of your creditors and it won't have the complete list of every company that's pulled your credit information for promotional purposes, like pre-approved credit card offers.

"If you compared the two reports side by side, the consumer one will have a couple more pages of information," says John Ulzheimer, president of consumer education with credit.com and former business development manager for myfico.com, a Web site of the Fair Isaac Corp. Fair Isaac is the creator of the FICO score, the widely known credit scoring model that is used to determine a person's credit risk.

Understanding the setup A credit report is basically divided into four sections: identifying information, credit history, public records and inquiries.

Identifying information is just that -- information to identify you. Look at it closely to make sure it's accurate. It's not unusual, Sweet says, for there to be two or three spellings of your name or more than one Social Security number. That's usually because someone reported the information that way. The variations will stay on your credit report; "If it's reported wrong, we leave it because it might mess up the link. Don't be concerned about variations."

Other information might include your current and previous addresses, your date of birth, telephone numbers, driver's license numbers, your employer and your spouse's name.

The next section is your credit history. Sometimes, the individual accounts are called trade lines.

Each account will include the name of the creditor and the account number, which may be scrambled for security purposes. You may have more than one account from a creditor. Many creditors have more than one kind of account, or if you move, they transfer your account to a new location and assign a new number.

The entry will also include:

» When you opened the account
» The kind of credit (installment, such as a mortgage or car loan, or revolving, such as a department store credit card)
» Whether the account is in your name alone or with another person
» Total amount of the loan, high credit limit or highest balance on the card

» How much you still owe
» Fixed monthly payments or minimum monthly amount
» Status of the account (open, inactive, closed, paid, etc.)
» How well you've paid the account

On Equifax's report, your payment history is written in plain English —never pays late, typically pays 30 days late, etc. Other comments might include internal collection and charged off or default.

"Charged off means the creditor has given up, thrown in the towel," Ulzheimer says. "He's made efforts to collect and written it off."

Other reports include color-coded payment legends. A green OK mark means the consumer is current on payments; a red PP designation means the debtor is on a payment plan. Numbers indicate how late a payment was.

The next section, public records, is the part you want to be absolutely blank. The public records section "is never a good story," Sweet says. "If you have a public record on there, you've had a problem."

It doesn't list arrests and criminal activities, just financial-related data, such as bankruptcies, judgments and tax liens. Those are the monsters that will trash your credit faster than anything else.

The final section is the inquiries. That's a list of everyone who asked to see your credit report.

"Any time anyone gets into the report, it'll post an inquiry," Ulzheimer says. "If you call the credit bureau and ask for a copy, it will be on there. It's a very detailed entry record. It's great for the consumer."

Inquiries are divided in different ways on different reports but they do distinguish hard pulls from soft pulls. "Hard" inquiries are ones you initiate by filling out a credit application. "Soft" inquiries are from companies that want to send out promotional information to a prequalified group or current creditors who are monitoring your account. The soft inquiries are only shown on reports given to consumers, according to Sweet.

You may have heard that a large number of inquiries can have a negative impact on your credit score, but you're probably OK.

"The vast majority of inquiries are ignored by the FICO scoring models," Ulzheimer says. "They're not the steak in the steak dinner."

For instance, the FICO scores ignore inquiries you request yourself. Rate shoppers need not fret either. The score counts two or more "hard" inquiries in the same 14-day period as just one inquiry.

"You could have 30 in two weeks and it only counts as one," Ulzheimer says.

Fixing mistakes If you find a mistake on your credit report -- an account that isn't yours or a disputed amount -- you'll need to fill out the form that comes with the report.

The process takes time because the creditors have 30 days to respond to a charge of a discrepancy, or 45 days if the dispute regards data in your free annual credit report. As long as a charge is in dispute, that dispute will show up on your report. Long-time lenders say it's common for reports to have errors. Some estimate that as many as 80 percent of all credit reports have some kind of misinformation.

Now, that you've read your report, dispute any mistakes you find by contacting each of the credit bureaus that report the error. Experian, TransUnion and Equifax allow you to do this online, but you may also submit your dispute by phone or mail.

If you suspect fraud, get a fraud alert placed on your credit file by contacting the fraud department of the credit bureau and explaining the situation. Alert other appropriate agencies as necessary.

While you can't delete negative but accurate and verifiable information, you can submit a 100-word consumer statement that explains the reason for the negative data. Your explanation will remain on your credit file until you remove it or until the data in dispute gets removed.

In the next chapter, I'm going to show you why a 401(k) might not be the best place for you to place any of your retirement dollars. You will be amazed at this information.

Chapter Seven

"Effective Saving Strategies"

$

I would like to introduce you to my humble definition of saving. Simply put, *"Saving is the storing up of items of importance for a time in the future when you will need access to them"*. I don't know what any dictionary says is the exact and correct definition, but this one proves itself time and again as we see more and more people who have no savings at all.

When people fail to put away money for times of economic difficulty, they are always the first to feel the pinch, and they often turn to using credit cards, or borrowing money to survive.

"But people who long to be rich fall into temptation and are trapped by many foolish and harmful desires that plunges them into ruin and destruction".

1st Timothy 6:9
—Life Application Study Bible

When we ask people today about their savings vehicles, we most often hear that they consider their 401(k) from their employer, or other "company sponsored" retirement program, to be their only savings vehicle, or tool.

These plans offer little or no protection, however, from the volatility of the stock market during challenging economic times, such as those we saw most recently in 2008. I believe that people have all but forgotten how to "SAVE." I'd like to introduce you to a little acronym I use when explaining what I mean by the term SAVE. Remember that whoever holds the money also holds the power to choose how it will be used.

Saving
- » Storing up items of importance, with a guarantee of increased value, for a time in the future when you decide you need access to them.
- » You retain control over, and access to these items.

Investing
- » Giving control of items of importance to others with a promise of higher financial reward, but no guarantees.
- » There is a risk of total loss associated with investing, but is tempting because of potentially high returns.

Please remember SAVE this way:
Safe
Accessible
Vehicle *that*
Empowers *the holder*

Far too many people get the term save confused with the term invest. Here is the difference:

I Timothy 6:9 from the Life Application Study Bible says, *"But people who long to be rich fall into temptation and are trapped by many foolish and harmful desires that plunges them into ruin and destruction."*

According to God's word, we must avoid those temptations that drive our ambitions for worldly riches, and decrease our opportunity for ruin and destruction. When we give away control of God's money, with which He has entrusted us, we are still going to be accountable for what happens to those gifts one day.

Maybe you have built a home, or witnessed the construction of a new building. You will always notice that there is detailed attention paid to the construction of the foundation of the structure. There must be a strong foundation to support the weight and stress that will be placed on the foundation. Without that firm and solid foundation, the structure stands little chance of long term survival. This philosophy also pertains to our financial foundation.

When we place our money in any environment that does not guarantee a positive return for us, we are intentionally placing cracks in the foundation of our financial future. If we place all our future retirement money, for example, into anything tied to the stock market, we are building the walls of the structure without a solid foundation. As a result, just like a home built with the walls built on sand, our financial future can be blown away with one strong storm.

I'd like to demonstrate for you the specifications of a strong, well built financial portfolio, which is designed to stand the test of time, and the strongest financial storms in economic history. You will recognize the shape of the structure because it is the same as some of the oldest structures on earth and represent a pyramid. The strong foundations of the great pyramids of Egypt have withstood thousands of years of war, storms, and weather. Because of their strong foundation, however, they stand strong and mighty today through the generations. If you want your wealth to be passed on and grown from generation to generation for your own family, follow this simple advice, and build your financial structure by the following blueprints. More details on how to use specific financial instruments will follow later, but remember this diagram.

A Blueprint for Financial Success!

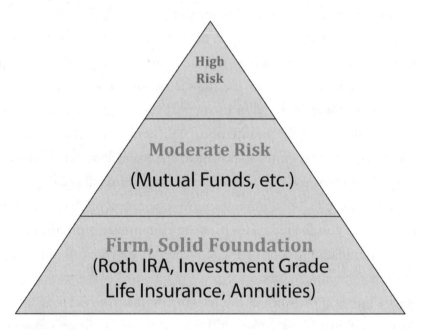

Whenever we attempt to understand effective ways to save money, we need to remember that whoever retains control over the assets also has the power to decide how the assets will be used, and often, when, and how, they can be accessed.

We briefly discussed control and access in Chapter 6, "Money Management," where we talked about the differences between sending extra money to the bank to pay down your mortgage, or to sending that money to a savings vehicle that earns compound interest for you.

The numbers showed us that you would save close to the same amount in interest, but the important thing is, *you* retain control over all your money, and have access to it if and when you ever need it, without having to try and borrow it back from the bank, which has the power to say no.

For millions of Americans who are investing money, where their money is and what it is being used for is a complete mystery. People receive monthly or quarterly statements, but don't know how to read them. They don't call to ask questions because they are too busy, or they don't want to appear ignorant about what is happening with their money.

It will enrich you to know that there are three phases of effective planning, in regard to saving. Each phase is just as important as the other two, but where you start your planning is probably the most important issue to keep in mind when you are working with your "Money Coach".

Three Phases of Saving

1. Contribution
2. Accumulation
3. Distribution

Most financial advisers or asset managers begin their planning from the first phase, are extremely interested in the second, but rarely interested in discussing the third phase. I'll explain to you what each phase is so that you will understand why their focus is almost always on the first two phases, and rarely on the third.

Contribution Phase:

This is the period of time when you take money from your paycheck while you're working, which will someday become the bedrock of your saving goals. Just like packing for a long trip to a place where you've never been, you're not sure exactly what you will need when you get there, but you want to make sure you pack everything you can think of to make life more comfortable. This is when we sacrifice accessibility to our money, and time with our family in an effort to earn enough to ensure a comfortable life after our working time is over. We typically miss children's recitals, ball games, and other family activities to make sure we've packed effectively.

Accumulation Phase:

This is the period of time when all your contributions grow by earning dividends or interest. This period of time can occur simultaneously with your contribution phase, and is like having someone help you pack for that long trip we just talked about. They are adding much needed essentials for your trip. It is extremely important to remember that, during this period of time, you need to be earning, and adding to your accounts, and not losing money!

Distribution Phase:

This is the period of time when you enjoy the fruits of your savings labor. This is when all the sacrifices seem worth it, if you've saved effectively.

This is the phase I believe is the most important one to begin planning from. If you begin your plan with the end in mind, you won't be surprised or disappointed when you get there. If you have designed a plan to provide beneficial tax elements for when you retire, and monitor this plan regularly, you shouldn't be surprised by unforeseen tax implications when you get there.

If, on the other hand, you blindly followed the masses, and placed all your money in pre-taxed investment programs, you may be in for a huge surprise when you reach retirement age. That's when your business partner, the Internal Revenue Service, will want all their money back that you deferred in taxes during your working life, plus interest.

Understanding all the different financial instruments, how they work, and how they are taxed is extremely important when you begin your savings plan.

This is the least favorite phase to your asset manager because this is when they stop getting paid on your money. Remember I told you that typical asset managers and investment advisers are more interested in the first two phases of your plan than the third? That's because we get paid during the first two, not the third phase.

I have a wonderful client in West Virginia who I adore. This 66 year old, single lady contacted me some time ago and was concerned about how to stretch her money to make it go a little farther. She was receiving an income from Social Security, along with a small pension from her former employer. She had retired about three years earlier, and had a mortgage payment and other living expenses.

As I was sitting with her, going over her assets and liabilities, she began to talk about another retirement account she had in a different state. She said her broker told her, however, that she should not access that money, but continue to pay her mortgage payment, and just make do with her tight budget.

When she told me that she had in excess of $260,000 in that account, I nearly fell out of my chair. This dear sweet retired lady was barely getting by while her asset manager was enjoying her retirement money!

I advised her to immediately liquidate that account, and open a single premium immediate fixed rate annuity. This would provide her with a guaranteed monthly income for the rest of her life, and she would never again have to worry about needing to stretch her money out to the end of the month.

She paid off her home, and is now enjoying her new life after a hip replacement. She is finally able to reap the rewards of her sacrifices over so many years, enjoying her own money instead of allowing her investment adviser to enjoy it.

When you develop a plan knowing when, and how, you want to access your money, make sure that when the time comes, you get the full benefit of all your hard work and sacrifice, instead of handing the benefits to someone else.

How to Use Different Financial Instruments

Of course you know a lottery is not a credible method of saving, but I had to throw it in because, a young couple, during their initial consultation with me some time ago, were actually counting on winning it to fund their retirement. I wasn't able to work with them as clients.

If you are serious about effective methods of saving, you shouldn't have to worry about which one of these, or any of the dozens of other options, would be the best choices for you.

You should depend on a Christian financial advisor (Money Coach) to advise you, and design a plan to fit your family's specific situation.

They work in this field every day, and are very familiar with the internal workings of all the best ways for you to accomplish your goals. For the purposes of this book, it isn't necessary to try and teach you about all the different financial tools available to you, because your "Money Coach" is already well versed on all aspects of them, and knows which ones will most benefit you.

Some Financial Tools

401K
Mutual Funds
403B
Stocks
IRA
Corporate Bonds
ROTH IRA
Treasury Bonds
SEP
Real Estate
Annuity
Commodities
Life Insurance
Lottery

Effective Saving Strategies

Most likely you wouldn't recognize Ted Benna. However, if you've had a job over the past 25 years or so, you will probably recognize his work. Ted Benna is a tax consultant hired by a large bank to find a legal way for them to get out of having to pay retirement or pension plans for their employees. He discovered a tax loophole that launched the now famous 401(k) tax-deferred investment accounts.

There are several quotes from a Time Magazine article dated September 20, 1980 with Mr. Benna that I want to share with you.

» "Seeking a tax break and an edge over its competitors, the bank wanted to replace its cash bonus plan with a deferred profit sharing plan under which employees wouldn't have access to the money until they left the bank"

» "I immediately realized it would be possible to change those plans so that employees would be able to put their money in before taxes rather than after"

» "I knew it wouldn't be attractive enough to get many of the lower paid employees to participate"

» "A bit of desperation got the creative juices flowing. That was when I thought of offering a matching employer contribution as an additional incentive. It was at this point that the potential of what I had just "created" hit"

» At the advice of their lawyers, **"The bank client rejected the idea."**

"Lower and middle income households, on the other hand, don't benefit as much from the program. They are less likely to be covered by any [pension] plan or by one that offers a generous company match. Since they pay lower tax rates, they get less out of the tax deferral. In all, about 70% of the tax benefits for 401(k) savings goes to the top 20% of earners. 'Given the way 401(k)s are structured, they are virtually designed to provide inadequate retirement income for the average worker."

—Jacob Hacker
Political Scientist
University of California-Berkley

Please do not get the wrong idea about 401(k) plans. When they are matched with an employer's dollars, they are a great supplemental retirement planning tool. In the absence of the employer match, however, they are just as the inventor of these plans stated, "It wouldn't be attractive enough."

There is absolutely no long term benefit to contributing pre-taxed dollars to a deferred compensation plan without an employer match. To substantiate these words, please review the following data.

If a 35 year old person contributed $200 per month for 30 years earning an 8% return, this is how the numbers would work:

401K with No Employer Match
» Amount of taxes you deferred while working $19,440
» Total accumulated value $243,994
» Taxes owed at withdrawal $72,745
» Your net Account Value $171,249

ROTH IRA
» Amount of taxes you deferred while working $0
» Total account value $243,994
» Taxes owed at withdrawal $0
» Your net account value $243,994

The problem is that we have been brainwashed to believe that if we don't put our money in the stock market, we'll never earn enough money to retire. This simply isn't true. The key is to be consistent, and committed, to a plan, and monitor results regularly. (See table 4)

Table 4

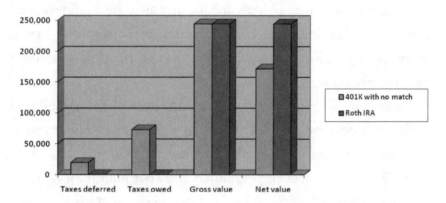

Let me give you an example of a situation just this past week. A gentleman called me and said he had placed $40,000 into a mutual fund for his son five years ago. Three months ago, he asked his asset manager to remove the funds from this investment and place them into an interest bearing account.

The asset manager failed to complete the trade, and the man lost over $3,000 of his original investment. He currently only had $37,000 of his original $40,000 investment left. He wanted to know what my recommendations were for his 11-year-old son. I recommended that we open a fixed-rate annuity earning 4.9% interest with a guaranteed minimum rate of 3%. After five years, the annuity will be earning 5.3%, but still with the minimum guarantee of 3%.

We let the money earn interest for five years in the annuity without touching it. After the five years, if they wanted to, he could start withdrawing $100 a month to invest in the stock market, in a mutual funds or another other suitable securities instrument, for 10 years, by utilizing a strategy called dollar cost averaging.

When we begin regular withdrawals of $1,200 per year, the client had $52,238 in his annuity, a $14,238 increase in five years, instead of a $3,000 decrease as a result of investing in the stock market. (See table 5)

We began regular withdrawals of $100 a month for 10 years. I chose the 10-year time frame because once the client is 26 years old, he will likely be working and contributing to his annuity. Allowing the annuity to grow for him without further withdrawals will take the account from $69,039 to $115,765 at the end of the next 10 years.

Table 5

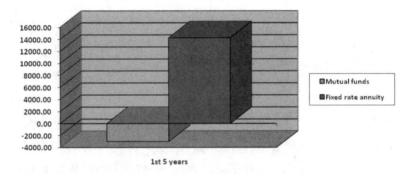

Here's the summary of what we did:

» Contributions from client: $37,000, placed in an interest-bearing, fixed-rate annuity with a guaranteed rate of return.

» Allow the initial contribution to earn interest for five years, growing to $52,238.

» After the fifth year, if desired and suitable, begin taking distributions equal to $100 per month from the annuity, and purchase securities-related investments, using the dollar cost averaging method, for 10 years.

» Even after regular withdrawals from the annuity for 10 years the annuity still has a value of $72,699.

» By the time the client is 36 years old, the original

contribution is worth $115,765, even after taking $12,000 out of the earnings within the first 15 years of the annuity.

» The $12,000 withdrawn has hopefully earned even more money through effective investing techniques.

» By the time the client is 65 years old, the original contribution of $37,000 has significantly increased to over $537,785, in addition to the $12,000 in withdrawals he invested to become an unknown amount, because no one can accurately predict what a return on investment will be in the stock market.

> **If you wouldn't gamble your family's grocery money on a blackjack table in Las Vegas, why would you gamble the money you'll depend on for groceries during retirement on Wall Street?**

What's the bottom line of saving versus investing? Always know what the return is on your foundational money, and review regularly to ensure you know where you are in regard to reaching your goals. The stock market doesn't provide the much needed predictability that is vital to being able to plan effectively. Even if that's what everyone else is doing, remember what your Mom used to say. "If all your friends were going to jump off a cliff, would you go and jump off, too?"

> **Be careful when you follow the herd—You might end up with what they leave behind**

There is a lot of wisdom in that statement. We don't have to follow the herd; in fact, if you have ever followed a herd of any type of animal, you've noticed that you have to closely watch your step, especially if you have on a new pair of shoes.

Now I'm ready to reveal the blueprints for the Trinity Plan. If you follow the steps laid out in the next few pages, you will never worry about losing the financial foundation with which God has blessed you. When called for an accounting, if you follow this plan, you will proudly give a good and positive report.

"A prudent person foresees the danger ahead and takes precautions. The simpleton goes blindly on and suffers the consequences". Proverbs 27:12 —Life Application Study Bible

With the Trinity Plan at your disposal, you will not have to go blindly.

The Trinity Plan

1. **Set aside three months of your family's expenses** in a money market account earning the best interest rate you can find at one of your local banks, or a bank you trust. Choose a money market account earning interest instead of a savings account because you typically receive a higher rate of return. Even if these accounts aren't paying high returns, it's still better than tucking it away under a mattress. Make sure you specify that you do not want this account tied to the stock market in any way! This is how the first part of the plan will look on the blueprint:

Money Market Account

2.   **Set aside an amount equal to one to three years of your family's total income** in an interest bearing Roth IRA, Fixed Rate Investment Grade Life Insurance, or a Fixed Rate Annuity, making sure the financial vehicle you choose is earning a good interest rate with a guaranteed return of at least 3%. I prefer investment-grade life insurance, if you are healthy enough to qualify.

3.   **Invest one third contribution from your income fund in an appropriate securities related instrument** (only after you have accomplished the first two goals), such as a mutual fund, and with the guidance of your money coach. **Every three months, make one contribution in this investment instrument**, implementing a strategy called "dollar cost averaging." Make sure you take a suitability test before placing any money into any securities related investment! A suitability test tells the financial advisor what your risk tolerance is, and gives them an idea of what type of investments are best suited for you at that particular time in your life. If the person you're entrusting your money to in the stock market has not given you one of these tests you should contact the appropriate authorities, because it is the law. The appropriate authority is FINRA (Financial Industry Regulatory Authority) website www.finra.org.

If you remember the basic diagram I laid out for you earlier in the book, you will notice we have taken it and plugged in the detailed information here that you will need to develop a successful financial plan.

I'm sure you're asking yourself right now, Who do I know who has followed such groundbreaking and radical thinking, especially in regard to life insurance as a financial tool?

In a day when every pundit on television and radio who feeds the masses information about where to place their money tells you to put everything into the stock market, why should you listen to the radical ideas I have laid out for you?

Am I sure this information is good advice that will really work? If only I knew someone who had followed this advice so I could ask them, you might say. I'd like to tell you about two individuals who took this advice and prospered.

Walt Disney

How about we ask "Uncle Walt" what he thinks. Walt Disney, as you all know, worked his entire life to bring enjoyment to others. Even after his death, we still enjoy what was once a vision. But how did he come up with the money to start such a huge empire? It is the stuff of legend in the financial industry exactly how he came up with the funds to start Disneyland: He took cash from his life insurance policy and mortgaged his home to make the down payment for what is now the Disney Empire.

Let's ask another very successful man what he thinks about putting all of your foundational money into the stock market. I recently saw an interview on the CNBC television network with Donald Trump, where he was asked, point blank, How much money do you have in the stock market? He replied, "Absolutely **no money** in the market because of the volatility."

Who is this man, you ask? How can anyone become so wealthy and not use the sound advice that is given to the masses that I have followed for so long? How can he be so wealthy, and what methods of money management does he follow?

I love the quote on his website. "We believe that there's more to mortgages than making a deal happen; it's about making a dream happen – your dream".

Donald Trump

One of the wealthiest men in America today uses some of the same financial strategies I have shown you in this book, but has $0 in the stock market.

Isn't it time for you to review how you are using God's money? Isn't it time to organize things in a way that will guarantee growth, stability, and accessibility? Isn't it time for you to ask yourself: If I had to give an account for how I have used God's money today, will I hear, "Well done, my good and faithful servant," or will I be cast out into the darkness and gnashing of teeth?

I hope you will contact one of our "Money Coaches today so they can help you start realizing your dreams. When you take your focus off of your money, you have more time to turn your focus toward serving God and growing His kingdom.

Imagine having the same money Donald Trump has, but using it for building God's kingdom, instead of a worldly one. You can do that by following the ideas and strategies that have been given to you in these pages.

Psalms 127:1:

"Unless the Lord builds a house, the work of the builders is wasted. Unless the Lord protects a city, guarding it with sentries will do no good." This verse tells me that if you build your wealth in a way that God blesses, He will protect it.

Chapter Eight

It's Five O'clock, Do You Know Where Your Money Is?

It's finally five o'clock on Friday. You've been working hard all week, and can't wait to get home to your family to enjoy some time together over the weekend. You got paid today so all the overtime you've put in seems worth it. As you glance at your pay stub, you realize all the deductions that came out, and you get frustrated.

But wait, you see your 401(k) contribution, and it makes you think of your retirement years when you won't have to work anymore. You see that in this pay period, you invested $235 in your retirement account. As you are getting off work, that money is going to work, too. But for whom is that money working? It's going to hopefully earn you a good return, but at what cost?

From a Biblical perspective, I Corinthians 6:9-1 (New Living translation) says: *"Don't you know that those who do wrong will have no share in the Kingdom of God? Don't fool yourselves. Those who indulge in sexual sin, who are idol worshipers, adulterers, male prostitutes, homosexuals, thieves, greedy people, drunkards, abusers and swindlers – none of these people will share in the Kingdom of God. There was a time when some of you were just like that, but now your sins have been washed away, and you have been set apart for God. You have been made right with God because of what the Lord Jesus Christ and the Spirit of our God have done for you."*

Even though it is clear in God's word that some people will not enter the Kingdom of Heaven, we all have the opportunity to turn from our evil ways and be made new in the sight of God, if we understand that there are behaviors that are wrong. There isn't any person who is created bad; we just choose to make bad decisions.

> For the commandments against adultery, and murder, and coveting - and any other commandment - are all summed up in this one commandment: "Love your neighbor as yourself."
> Romans 13:9
> —Application Study Bible

If you are, have been, or know a homosexual or anyone else who falls into this category, I want you to know that I pray that they will undergo the same transformation I did.

Because I was an adulterer, I would not have had the opportunity to enter God's Kingdom, but I was given the chance to change my behavior so that I could be useful to Him. By God's grace I am saved.

The only thing that separates me from the most heinous criminal and sinner living today is the fact that I accepted God's mercy when offered. I pray that everyone else will accept His mercy, because that's what He desires for everyone.

No matter the behavior, we must love everyone as ourselves. Jesus demands that we love the sinner, not the sin. Pray for those who need God's mercy and forgiveness, just as I needed it. Eternity is a long time!

When you make an automatic contribution to your retirement plan, do you know where that money goes from there? You might be surprised to see that some of your money is being invested, and spent, in ways that you would never approve of, in places you would never dream of going, and in vulgar materials that you would never think of reading.

You might even be unknowingly funding the trafficking of innocent women and children for the sex slave market in Asian countries through mutual funds listed as "Emerging Markets" or some "International Funds." These mutual funds send your hard earned money directly to companies owned and operated in countries such as China and India. These countries don't mind taking our money for their purposes, but have you ever tried to preach Christianity, or give away Bibles in a public square in Beijing?

Since most people invest in mutual funds through their retirement plans because of a perception of reduced risk, let's take a quick look at how a mutual fund works. When your employer collects that money from your pay, they forward it on to the asset manager in charge of your account. He or she sends it on to the broker/dealer, who then directs your money to the fund management company that distributes those funds to the appropriate companies in exchange for a partial share of ownership.

Those companies use some of your money for their operating budget, advertising budget, or administrative budget. Let's say that you had $3 that actually made it to ABC Company. One dollar might go to each of the three divisions we just spoke of.

The operating budget is where one of your dollars will get put to work paying the salary of employees, including executives, or purchasing new equipment that will enhance business. The administrative budget is where your second dollar is put to work buying paper that will serve as memos announcing important safety meetings, office parties, or reports to shareholders. It might also be used to fund management retreats at luxury spas, or attracting and entertaining potential clients. Then there is the advertising budget.

This is the area where most people fail to see what damage their third dollar is being used for. This damage isn't any more evident than the damage what many companies today cause in seeking to attract the $510 billion that is up for grabs from the homosexual market in 2008(Say what year. Is this statistic current?), according to the Gay Friendly Network (www.gfn.com).

GFN claims that there are approximately 15 million gay Americans who have money to invest, and the financial service companies are fighting for those dollars with advertising money obtained from your retirement account. If you want to learn more about the buying power of the "gay friendly" market, visit GFN's website and read the media report for yourself (gfn.com/documents/GFNMedia).

You will absolutely be amazed at how successful this incredible marketing program has been in attracting money from relatively good companies to promote their agenda. Look at the list of advertisers who buy advertising in *The Advocate*, a gay magazine (advocate.com). You can verify anything I say from these links.

When you look at the companies that are advertising in "The Advocate," you will see that there is an organization by the name of GFN (the Gay Friendly Network). The home page to this organization is gfn.com, and their website about their financial status that lists some of their advertisers (gfn.com/documents/ GFNMedia): American Express, IBM, US Airways, Conseco, MetLife Bank, E-Loan, and Quicken Loans, to mention just a few.

Let's take a look at one company you might have in your retirement account without even knowing it. One of these "advertising partners" loves gay dollars so much they spend your retirement dollars to get them. Does your 401 (k) include a mutual fund that invests in IBM? Very likely, it does.

Did any of your retirement money pay for this?

IBM is one of the most commonly held companies in mutual funds seeking long term returns for their investors. In a five-minute search, I found that Fidelity Funds held IBM in two fund families, and Vanguard held IBM in seven of their fund families. I don't wish to single out these fund companies, because other funds include IBM, but these good companies are just the first ones I came across when I conducted my brief experiment. These are both widely held mutual fund companies in the retirement planning arena.

If you are interested in finding out where your dollars are going from your retirement plan, contact your asset manager today. Ask them what companies are using your money – no, I mean God's money. If you don't know where your money is, and what it's being used for, you will be the one who has to account for your choices one day.

You can correct this problem by using only Christian financial professionals who specialize in "faith based investing." One such mutual fund that only invests in companies who advertise and allocate funds for the use of godly programs is "The Timothy Plan. A Christian financial professional certified as a "Money Coach" will be able to assist you with finding more information on these funds, as well as others that might be available as an alternative to secular investing, where your dollars are used to fund agendas you don't want to support.

For your convenience, here is a chart that tracks your money as it relates to investing in promoting the homosexual agenda.

Is this the Flow of Your Money?

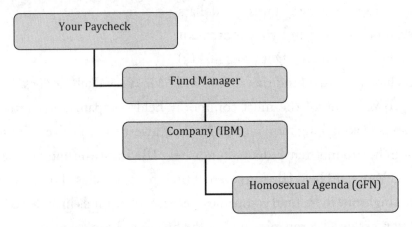

I hope this information will cause you to take a closer look at exactly where you are sending God's money. If He handed that money directly to you, would you be as careless with it if you knew where your money was going? Or would you research exactly what that money would be used to support, and invest according to God's will? This is just another example of how following the masses is destroying our nation, our families, and diverting us from our desire to further our relationship with God.

Remember what I said earlier: You can tell where someone's focus is by looking at how they spend their money. I want to believe that your focus isn't on earning a high return for your money over supporting God's kingdom, but I haven't seen your 401K statement. God has seen that statement!

I can't blame homosexuals for trying to collect these advertising dollars; in fact, I applaud them for their efforts to attract our hard-earned money. We should take a lesson from their playbook, though. When the "gay rights" people organize a boycott of a certain business, those businesses usually give in to their demands, because they know that, otherwise, they may lose that particular market.

If they don't take a stand, they can gain the business of the homosexuals, and they won't lose the business of the Christians. It's a win-win situation for them.

By not giving in, they retain their Christian customers, and money from the homosexual agenda doesn't go to a competitor.

If, however, businesses knew they would lose the larger market share of Christians seeking to do the right thing, they might take a closer look before caving in to the special interest groups. What are we doing to send that message out? How are we conveying our message to corporate America that we will not stand for this behavior? The American Family Association (AFA) is one organization that was bold enough to take that stand for your family. They boycotted such companies as Ford motor company and McDonalds, using their organization to enlist the support of millions to join them in this stand for godly responsibility.

As a result, both Ford and McDonalds sent messages to AFA announcing that they made changes in response of these boycotts.

Other large corporations will listen and react favorably if we let them know where we stand. Companies will be more responsible when they know they will not have access to your money. Worldly priorities cause people of the world to take the actions they do. If you are dedicated to serving God, and being a good steward of His money, you will act to make a significant change in the way you view and use money.

Take that first step today by contacting a "Money Coach" who has been certified by the Abundant Life Institute, and have them design and implement a financial strategy for you and your family that will be pleasing to God. The easiest way to do this is to attend one of our free Financial Empowerment Workshops in your area. All this information is available to you on our website, which is Godsdollar.com.

Send a message through how you invest and spend your money to corporate America. Tell them through your investing and spending habits that you choose to support God's kingdom, not theirs. Tell them what the prophet said in **Joshua 24:15:**

"But if serving the Lord seems undesirable to you, then choose for yourselves this day whom you will serve, whether the gods your forefathers served beyond the River, or the gods of the Amorites, in whose land you are living. But as for me and my household, we will serve the Lord."

As we come to the close of this book, I realize that I haven't mentioned my hero in quite a while. I'd like to end this book with a story I once heard Rev. John Maxwell tell. I may not tell the story in Dr. Maxwell's exact words, but the message is the same.

It seems that there was a traveler who made a point of stopping in each small town he came across during his trek across America in an effort to learn more about that town's claim to fame, or what it was noted for.

The traveler stopped in this one small town and noticed an elderly gentleman sitting on a bench in front of the local general store whittling on a piece of wood. The traveler greeted the man, and asked him what this town was noted for. The man said "nothing really". The traveler asked him, you mean there's nothing special about this lovely little town that you want me to know about? The man looked up at him and said:

I guess the one thing that makes us special is that you can get to anywhere you want to be from right here. No matter where you've been before, this is the starting place for anywhere in the world you want to go.

I believe that statement stands true with your financial and for your spiritual status as well. No matter where you've been before, this is the starting place for where ever in the world you want to go. It all starts now. Will you continue to follow the path of the world, or will you begin walking in the path that will glorify God, and bring you blessings from Him?

Now that you have read this book, I realize that you might be interested in talking to a Money Coach, or interested in learning more about becoming a Money Coach. For your convenience I have listed the criteria required to be able to assist us in this program as a certified Money Coach. For more information you should contact us at **www.godsdollar.com.**

Money Coach Certification Criteria

» Applicant must have a minimum of two years of fulltime employment as a financial advisor, consultant, or planner.

» Applicant must possess, and maintain, a current life insurance license issued from the state(s) in which they intend to conduct business.

» Applicant must hold at least a series 6 and 63 license through FINRA.

» Applicant cannot have had any disciplinary actions or sanctions by any department of insurance, or banking commission in any state, or with the Securities and Exchange Commission, the federal agency that regulates the securities industry.

» Applicant must provide a letter of recommendation from the leader of their place of worship, or a written statement of their faith.

» You must be willing to pray with and for those who come to you for help through this ministry.

Family Financial Goal Sheet

"A Goal is But a Dream, Until You Write It Down"

Name: _____

Age: _____

Spouse: _____

Age: _____

Address: _____

City: _____

State: _____ Zip: _____

Home Phone: _____

E-Mail: _____

Your Short Term (6 – 24 months) Goals / Concerns:

1. _____

_____

2. _____

_____

3. _____

_____

Your Mid-Range (2 – 5 years) Goals / Concerns:

1. _____

_____

2. _____

_____

3. _____

_____

Your Long Term (years 5 and beyond) Goals / Concerns:

1. _____

_____

2. _____

_____

3. _____

_____

Current monthly income: Male_____ Female_____

At what age do you plan to retire? Male_____ Female _____

Desired total monthly income at retirement? _____

Index

Sample
Presentation

Financial Needs Analysis

John and Jane Doe

**35 Abrams Dr
Your Town, MO 65616**

Presented by:
The Abundant Life Institute

Introduction

When thinking about your future financial security, it is important to set goals, initiate action, and periodically review your progress.

Remember...a sound financial strategy can be more important than a lifetime of work!

This analysis uses the information you have shared about your current financial situation and your goals for the future.

The following pages analyze your needs:

- In the event of death
- For college funding
- For your retirement years
- For your asset allocation
- In the event of a disability

Understanding your needs

...can help reach your goals.

Important Note...

This illustration is based on the information you provided with regard to your financial needs and objectives. It is intended to provide only broad, general guidelines which may be helpful in assessing and making decisions about financial products (such as securities or insurance) and services available to you that may help meet those needs and objectives. This material may also contain general educational topics about investing and financial matters. It is most important that you understand that your actual experience will differ from this illustration. That is why you should reassess your situation with updated data and assumptions on a periodic basis.

This illustration estimates future asset values based on rates of return provided by you. It is not intended to be investment advice or a projection of future investment performance. No one can foresee the future and, it is not a projection of the potential return of any investment, nor is it a projection of future inflation rates or the state of the world or domestic economy. You should seek the guidance of a financial or investment professional before proceeding with an investment decision.

Although this illustration may contain income tax calculations and legal concepts, it does not constitute tax or legal advice. The application of some concepts may be considered practicing law and should, therefore, be handled by an attorney, while other concepts may require the guidance of a tax or accounting advisor.

Continued...

Presented by: The Abundant Life Institute

In creating the illustration certain assumptions were made with respect to investment returns, the economy, and your situation. The reports and graphics included are directly dependent on the quality and the accuracy of the data and assumptions (including rates of return) furnished by you.

Where future rates of return are assumed, these returns do not reflect the fees and charges associated with investments, which would reduce the results. You are encouraged to review and consider performance information, which you can request from your investment professional, for the mutual funds and other securities that may be referenced in this material when assuming any future rates of return. Keep in mind that past performance is not a guarantee of future results. A current prospectus must be read carefully when considering any investment in securities.

No liability is assumed resulting from the use of the information contained in this financial illustration. Responsibilities for financial decisions are assumed by you.

Presented by: The Abundant Life Institute

Personal Information Summary

This financial needs analysis report is based on the information and assumptions you provided.

Personal Data

Name	Date of Birth	Contributing to Social Security	Annual Employment Income
John Doe	8/11/1967	Yes	$87,500
Jane Doe	8/9/1970	Yes	$42,500

Married: Yes

Address
35 Abrams Dr
Your Town, MO 65616   *Phone:*   (555) 555-5555

E-Mail   Janedoe@HOTMAIL.COM

Children

Name	Date of Birth
Sarah	5/14/2008

Asset Allocation

Time Horizon		Risk Tolerance	
Question 1:	f. 11 years or more	Question 3:	c. Portfolio 3
Question 2:	e. 11 years or more	Question 4:	a. Portfolio A
		Question 5:	b. Keep risk to a minimum
		Question 6:	c. Wait at least 3 months before changing
		Question 7:	d. Portfolio D
Suggested Portfolio:	Low Risk/Return	Question 8:	c. Strongly Disagree

Bank Accounts and Investments

Owner	Account Name	Asset Name	Ticker	Amount	Rate of Return	Monthly Savings	Savings Increase	Asset Class
				$0	0.00%	$0	0.00%	
Both		CD		$23,000	4.70%	$0	0.00%	Unclassified
Both		I Bond		$3,000	4.75%	$0	0.00%	Unclassified
Both		Money Market 2		$27,224	2.75%	$0	0.00%	Unclassified
Jane		Money Market		$13,668	2.75%	$0	0.00%	Unclassified
John		Money Market 3		$10,000	2.75%	$0	0.00%	Unclassified
Both				$0	0.00%	$0	0.00%	Unclassified

Total............................. $76,892
Monthly Savings................. $0
Average Rate of Return...........   3.41%

Retirement Funds

Owner	Account Name	Asset Name	Ticker	Amount	Rate of Return	Monthly Savings	Savings Increase	Company Match	Asset Class
				$0	0.00%	$0	0.00%	$0	Unclassified
Jane		Blended Acct		$32,134	2.00%	$0	0.00%	$0	Unclassified
Jane		Current 401K		$7,871	0.00%	$150	0.00%	$100	Unclassified
Jane		Old 401K		$34,971	2.00%	$0	0.00%	$0	Unclassified
John		401K		$25,000	2.00%	$260	0.00%	$206	Unclassified
John		IRA		$21,000	4.50%	$0	0.00%	$0	Unclassified

Continued...

Total......	$120,976
Monthly Savings.....	$410
Average Rate of Return...	2.30%

Assets and Liabilities

Type	Name	Market Value	Current Liability	Monthly Payment	Interest Rate
Real Estate	Condo	$220,000	$218,000	$0	0.00%
Residence	Mortgage	$190,000	$110,000	$645	4.80%
Credit Cards & Personal Loans		$0	$0	$0	0.00%
Credit Cards & Personal Loans	Car	$0	$9,500	$220	5.25%

Other Income Sources

Name	Description	Amount	Monthly/ Lump Sum	Begins at Age	Ends at Age	Annual Increase	Today's Value/ Future Value	Available for Survivors
John	Condo	$667	Monthly	41	90	3.00%	Today's	Yes

Needs In The Event Of Death

Income Needs Objective	With children at home: 70.00%	No children at home: 50.00%
Provide Income for	Lifetime	
Fund Children's Education	Yes	

Life Insurance Policies

Name	Company	Insurance Benefit	Annual Premium	Type
John		$360,000	$0	
Jane		$10,000	$0	

College Funding

Child's Name	School	Annual Amount (in Today's Dollars)	Years Needed	Percent Want To Provide
Sarah		$0	4	100%

Total Funds Presently Available	Monthly Savings	Rate of Return
$0	$0	5.00%

Retirement Needs

	John	Jane
Desired Retirement Age	65	65
Social Security Retirement Benefits Begin Age	67	67
Employer Offers Retirement Plans	Yes	Yes
Maximum amount being contributed	No	No
Percentage of pre-retirement income during retirement	80.00%	

Long-Term Disability

Annual Employment Income	$87,500	$42,500
Disability income replacement objective:	John - 60.00%	Jane - 60.00%

Existing Insurance

Insured	Company	Monthly Benefit	Group/ Personal	Annual Premium	Waiting Period (Months)	Benefit Period
Jane		$600	Group	$240	1 month	3 months

Continued...

Presented by: The Abundant Life Institute

Assumptions Used In This Analysis

Rate of Return on Assets

During Retirement	5.00%
In the Event of Death	5.00%
For College Needs	5.00%
Number of month's income to set aside for	
emergency reserves	3
Long-term inflation rate	4.00%
Social Security inflation rate	2.50%
Long-term inflation rate for College Costs	6.00%
Life expectancy age	90
Final Expenses	$10,000

Presented by: The Abundant Life Institute

Net Worth

Assets	Owner	ROR	Market Value
Bank Accounts and Investments			
CD	Both	4.70%	$23,000
I Bond	Both	4.75%	3,000
Money Market 2	Both	2.75%	27,224
Money Market	Jane	2.75%	13,668
Money Market 3	John	2.75%	10,000
Retirement Plans			
Blended Acct	Jane	2.00%	32,134
Current 401K	Jane	0.00%	7,871
Old 401K	Jane	2.00%	34,971
401K	John	2.00%	25,000
IRA	John	4.50%	21,000
Residence			
Mortgage	Both	--	190,000
Real Estate			
Condo	Both	--	220,000
Total Assets			**$607,868**

Liabilities	Owner	Interest Rate	Liability Value
Residence			
Mortgage	Both	4.80%	(110,000)
Real Estate			
Condo	Both	N/A	(218,000)
Credit Cards & Personal Loans			
Car	Both	5.25%	(9,500)
Total Liabilities			**($337,500)**

Net Worth			**$270,368**

Presented by: The Abundant Life Institute

Notes

Client Objectives

This Analysis Addresses the Following Goals

Recommendations
The Following Changes Are Recommended

Presented by: The Abundant Life Institute

Retirement Needs Analysis

Will you have enough money when you retire? The earlier you begin setting money aside, the more likely you are to achieve your retirement goals.

Retirement income generally comes from three different sources:

- *Social Security*
- *Employer Sponsored Plans*
- *Savings and Investments*

*This retirement analysis suggests that you might not have enough money to retire. It is estimated that your assets will be **depleted** by age 69. At that time, your remaining income sources will be limited to Social Security and Other Income sources, providing only 23% of your income.*

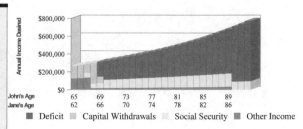

To provide for your desired retirement income, you will need additional capital at retirement age 65. In order to meet this need, you should consider:

- Saving more money
- Earning a higher return on your assets

If you are not able to accumulate this capital, you may need to consider:

- Postponing your retirement, or
- Reducing your standard of living

This chart shows various options in order for you to meet your objectives. Based on your current average rate of return of 2.44%, you would need to save an additional $9,761 a month. Alternatively, if you could increase your average rate of return to 11.97%, your objectives would be met. It is important to understand that in order to achieve an increased rate of return, it is likely you will face increased risk.

If these options are not attainable, work towards doing a little bit of both; saving more money and earning a higher rate of return.

Assumptions: Income increases at 4.00% annually. Rate of return during retirement is 5.00%. Social Security benefits increase at 2.50%.

Retirement Needs Analysis Detail

Income Objective

	Current Household Income	Annual Need (Today's Dollars)	Annual Need (At Retirement)	Capital Value
At John's Age 65	$130,000	$104,000	$266,584	$6,434,485

Total Value of Income Objective   **$6,434,485**

Income Sources

Income Sources	Payment In Today's Dollars	From	To	COLA	First Year's Payment	Capital Value
Jane's Employment	$42,500	62	65	4.00%	$108,940	$316,591
John's Social Security	27,181	67	90	2.50%	51,651	818,798
Jane's Social Security	18,588	67	90	2.50%	38,039	545,275
Condo	8,004	65	90	3.00%	16,270	318,871

Total Income Sources   **$1,999,535**

Capital Needed to Meet Objectives $4,434,950

Capital Available

Account Name/ Asset Name	Market Value	Assumed Rate of Return	Total Annual Contribution	Assumed Savings Increase	Value At Retirement
Blended Acct	$32,134	2.00%	$0	0.00%	$47,381
Current 401K	7,871	0.00%	3,000	0.00%	76,770
Old 401K	34,971	2.00%	0	0.00%	51,564
401K	25,000	2.00%	5,592	0.00%	212,167
IRA	21,000	4.50%	0	0.00%	60,396
CD	23,000	4.70%	0	0.00%	69,255
I Bond	3,000	4.75%	0	0.00%	9,137
Money Market 2	27,224	2.75%	0	0.00%	52,205
Money Market	13,668	2.75%	0	0.00%	24,561
Money Market 3	10,000	2.75%	0	0.00%	19,176
Total Capital Available					**$622,613**

Additional Capital Needed to Meet Objectives $3,812,337

Assumptions

Income Replacement at Retirement in the year 2033   80%

Continued...

Inflation	4.00%
Rate of Return for Assets during Retirement	5.00%
Mortality assumed for John and Jane	90 / 90

Presented by: The Abundant Life Institute

Your Retirement Timeline

					Beginning Balance:	**$622,613**
John's Age	*Jane's Age*	*Annual Income Desired*	*Social Security*	*Other Income*	*Interest And Dividends*	*Balance*
65	62	$266,584	$0	$125,211	$27,330	$508,570
66	63	277,247	0	130,057	21,472	382,852
67	64	288,337	51,651	135,091	16,412	297,669
68	65	299,870	52,943	17,779	8,724	77,245
69	66	311,865	54,266	18,313	(2,570)	(164,612)
70	67	324,340	93,662	18,862	(13,925)	(390,352)
71	68	337,313	96,003	19,428	(25,482)	(637,716)
72	69	350,806	98,403	20,011	(38,133)	(908,241)
73	70	364,838	100,864	20,611	(51,954)	(1,203,559)
74	71	379,432	103,385	21,229	(67,028)	(1,525,404)
75	72	394,609	105,970	21,866	(83,441)	(1,875,618)
76	73	410,393	108,619	22,522	(101,288)	(2,256,158)
77	74	426,809	111,335	23,198	(120,665)	(2,669,099)
78	75	443,881	114,118	23,894	(141,677)	(3,116,646)
79	76	461,637	116,971	24,611	(164,436)	(3,601,137)
80	77	480,102	119,895	25,349	(189,058)	(4,125,053)
81	78	499,306	122,892	26,109	(215,669)	(4,691,027)
82	79	519,278	125,965	26,893	(244,401)	(5,301,849)
83	80	540,050	129,114	27,699	(275,394)	(5,960,480)
84	81	561,652	132,342	28,530	(308,798)	(6,670,057)
85	82	584,118	135,650	29,386	(344,768)	(7,433,906)
86	83	607,482	139,042	30,268	(383,474)	(8,255,553)
87	84	631,782	142,518	31,176	(425,092)	(9,138,733)
88	85	657,053	146,081	32,111	(469,809)	(10,087,403)
89	86	683,335	149,733	33,075	(517,825)	(11,105,756)
--	87	710,668	91,145	0	(571,941)	(12,297,221)
--	88	739,095	93,423	0	(632,218)	(13,575,110)
--	89	768,659	95,759	0	(696,844)	(14,944,854)

Presented by: The Abundant Life Institute

Pay Yourself First

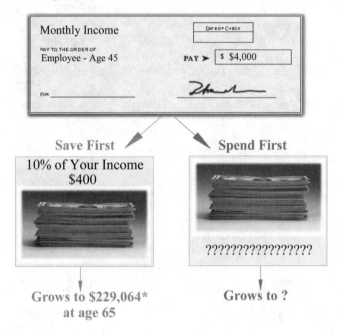

Do you save first or spend first?

* This is a hypothetical example for illustrative purposes and is not indicative of any
investment. Investments involve risks that could result in the loss of principal. There is no
guarantee that the strategy illustrated will produce positive investment results. This example
assumes payroll deductions of $400 per month for the next 20 years growing at an assumed rate
of return of 8.00%.

Retirement Statistics

According to recent government statistics, incomes for people age 65 and older are:

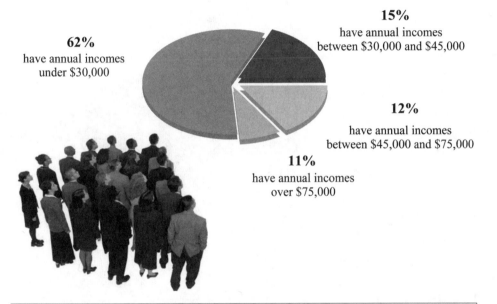

62%
have annual incomes
under $30,000

15%
have annual incomes
between $30,000 and $45,000

12%
have annual incomes
between $45,000 and $75,000

11%
have annual incomes
over $75,000

Most people are very concerned about their prospect for retirement. Over 70% believe they won't have enough money at retirement. Of those between the ages of 30 and 54, almost 80% feel this way.

One of the factors in their uncertainty is Social Security. In the mid-1970s, two-thirds of those surveyed said they were confident that Social Security benefits would be there for them at retirement. In the 1980s this was completely reversed. Two-thirds said they were not confident that Social Security would be there at retirement, and if it were, it would not be adequate to provide a reasonable standard of living.

There does, however, seem to be agreement that being financially independent at retirement requires putting money aside while you're working and earning income...even if it means making some short-term sacrifices along the way.

Source: Social Security Administration, The Office of Policy, Income of the Population 55 or older 2006, table 3.1; released Feb. 2009.

Asset Allocation: Current vs. Recommended

Based on your tolerance for risk and the timeframe in which you need to use the invested funds, you are considered a Conservative Investor.

This type of investor is particularly sensitive to short-term losses, but still has the likely goal of beating expected inflation over the long run. There should be growth in the real value of assets over the long run.

Your Current Portfolio   Low Risk/Return Portfolio

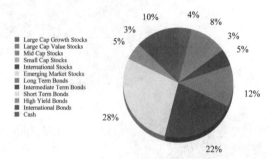

- Large Cap Growth Stocks
- Large Cap Value Stocks
- Mid Cap Stocks
- Small Cap Stocks
- International Stocks
- Emerging Market Stocks
- Long Term Bonds
- Intermediate Term Bonds
- Short Term Bonds
- High Yield Bonds
- International Bonds
- Cash

All investments contain some form and degree of risk that investors should carefully consider prior to investing. Upon redemption, the principal value of investments in stocks and bonds may be worth more or less than when purchased. Small company stocks may be subject to a higher degree of market and liquidity risk than the stocks of larger companies. Investments in foreign stocks are subject to additional risks (e.g., foreign taxation, economic and political risks) and these risks can be accentuated in emerging markets. Bond prices will drop as interest rates rise. High yield bonds are more susceptible to certain risks (e.g., credit risk, default risk) and are more volatile than investment grade bonds.

Benchmark Descriptions

Large Cap Growth Stocks - Russell 1000 ® Growth Index
The Russell 1000 Growth Index contains those Russell 1000 securities with a greater-than-average growth orientation. Companies in this index tend to exhibit higher price-to-book and price-earnings ratios, lower dividend yields and higher forecasted growth values than the Value universe.

Large Cap Value Stocks - Russell 1000 ® Value Index
The Russell 1000 Value Index contains those Russell 1000 securities with a less-than-average growth orientation. Securities in this index generally have lower price-to-book and price-earnings ratios, higher dividend yields and lower forecasted growth values than the Growth universe.

Mid Cap Stocks - Russell Midcap ® Index
The Russell Mid Cap Index consists of the smallest 800 companies in the Russell 1000 index, as ranked by total market capitalization. This midcap index represents approximately 31% of the Russell 1000 total market capitalization. As of January 2009, the average market capitalization was approximately $5.024 billion; the median market capitalization was approximately $2.254 billion. The largest company in the index had an approximate market capitalization of $13.815 billion.

Small Cap Stocks - Russell 2000 ® Index
The Russell 2000 Index is a small-cap index consisting of the smallest 2,000 companies in the Russell 3000 Index, representing approximately 10% of the Russell 3000 ® total market capitalization. As of January 2009, the average market capitalization was approximately $0.823 billion; the median market capitalization was approximately $0.277 billion. The largest company in the index had an approximate market capitalization of $3.329 billion.

International Stocks - MSCI EAFE ® Index
The MSCI EAFE (Europe, Australasia, Far East) Index is a free float-adjusted market capitalization index that is designed to measure developed market equity performance, excluding the US & Canada. As of January 2009 the MSCI EAFE Index consisted of the following 21 developed market country indices: Australia, Austria, Belgium, Denmark, Finland, France, Germany, Greece, Hong Kong, Ireland, Italy, Japan, the Netherlands, New Zealand, Norway, Portugal, Singapore, Spain, Sweden, Switzerland and the United Kingdom. The index is maintained by Morgan Stanley Capital International which aims to include 60% coverage of the total market capitalization for each market.

Emerging Market Stocks - MSCI Emerging Markets Index
The MSCI Emerging Markets Index is a free float-adjusted market capitalization index that is designed to measure equity market performance in the global emerging markets. As of January 2009 the MSCI Emerging Markets Index consisted of the following 23 emerging market country indices: Argentina, Brazil, Chile, China, Colombia, Czech Republic, Egypt, Hungary, India, Indonesia, Israel, Korea, Malaysia, Mexico, Morocco, Peru, Philippines, Poland, Russia, South Africa, Taiwan, Thailand and Turkey.

Long-Term Bonds - US Long-Term Government Bonds
The objective of this benchmark is to measure the returns of long-term bonds. To the greatest extent possible the total returns are calculated for each year on a single bond issued by the United States Government with a term of approximately 20 years and a reasonably current coupon with returns that did not reflect potential tax benefits, impaired negotiability, or special redemption or call privileges.

Continued...

Presented by: The Abundant Life Institute

Intermediate Term Bonds - US Intermediate Term Government Bonds

The objective of this benchmark is to measure the returns of intermediate-term bonds. As with long-term government bonds, one-bond portfolios are used to construct the intermediate-term index. The bond chosen each year is the shortest non-callable bond with a maturity of not less than five years, and it is "held" for the calendar year. Monthly returns are computed. Bonds with impaired negotiability or special redemption privileges are omitted, as are partially or fully tax-exempt bonds starting in 1943.

Short-Term Bonds - US 1-Year Government Bonds

The objective of this benchmark is to reflect the returns provided by the short-term fixed income instruments. Yields on Treasury securities at "constant maturity" are interpolated by the U.S. Treasury from the daily yield curve. This curve, which relates the yield on a security to its time to maturity, is based on the closing market bid yields on actively traded Treasury securities in the over-the-counter market. These market yields are calculated from composites of quotations obtained by the Federal Reserve Bank of New York. The constant maturity yield values are read from the yield curve at fixed maturities, currently 3 and 6 months and 1, 2, 3, 5, 7, 10, 20 and 30 years. This method provides a yield for a 10-year maturity, for example, even if no outstanding security has exactly 10 years remaining to maturity.

> From the yield that is provided by the U.S. Treasury, the following are calculated:
> Total Return = (ending flat price)/(beginning flat price) -1
> Beginning flat price = 100 * (1-(lagged decimal yield)*30/360)
> Ending flat price = 100

High Yield Bonds - Barclay's High Yield Index

The BarCap High Yield Index covers the universe of fixed rate, noninvestment grade debt. Criteria to be included in the index are as follows:

1. All bonds must be dollar-denominated and nonconvertible.
2. All bonds must have at least one year remaining to maturity and an outstanding par value of at least $100 million. (Limit of $100 million was raised from $50 million in January 1993.)
3. Pay-in-kind (PIK) bonds, Eurobonds, and debt issues from countries designated as emerging markets are excluded, but Yankee and global bonds (SEC registered) of issuers in non-emerging countries are included.
4. Original issue zeroes and step-up coupon structures are also included.

In general, all securities must be rated Ba1or lower by Moody's Investors Service, including defaulted issues. If no Moody's rating is available, bonds must be rated BB+ or lower by S&P; and if no S&P rating is available, bonds must be rated below investment grade by Fitch Investor's Service.

A small number of unrated bonds are included in the index; to be eligible they must have previously held a high yield rating or have been associated with a high yield issuer, and must trade accordingly. In 1998, 144A securities were added to this index.

International Bonds - Citigroup WGBI Non-U.S.

The objective of this benchmark is to reflect the returns provided by investment in international (non U.S.) fixed income securities. The World Government Bond Index is a market-capitalization weighted benchmark that tracks the performance of fixed-rate sovereign debt issued in the domestic market in the local currency with at least one year maturity. The minimum credit quality required is BBB-/Baa3 (by either S&P or Moody's) for all issuers to ensure that the WGBI remains an investment-grade benchmark.

Continued...

Presented by: The Abundant Life Institute

Cash - Citigroup US Domestic 3 Month T-Bill

The objective of this benchmark is to reflect the returns provided by the short term fixed income instruments. The index is based on the U.S. 3 month Treasury Bills. This index measures monthly return equivalents of yield averages that are not marked to market. Calculations are based on the last 3, 3-month T-Bill issues. Returns for this index are then calculated on a monthly basis.

Presented by: The Abundant Life Institute

What is Asset Allocation?

Asset allocation is the process of developing a diversified portfolio by combining different assets in varying proportions.

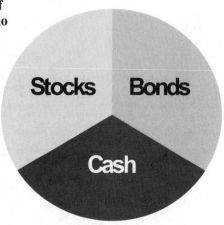

What is Asset Allocation?

The asset allocation decision is one of the most important factors in determining both the return and the risk of an investment portfolio.

Asset allocation is the process of developing a diversified investment portfolio by combining different assets in varying proportions.

An asset is anything that produces income or can be purchased and sold, such as stocks, bonds, or certificates of deposit (CDs). Asset classes are groupings of assets with similar characteristics and properties. Examples of asset classes are large-company stocks, long-term government bonds, and Treasury bills.

Every asset class has distinct characteristics and may perform differently in response to market changes. Therefore, careful consideration must be given to determine which assets you should hold and the amount you should allocate to each asset.

Factors that greatly influence the asset allocation decision are your financial needs and goals, the length of your investment horizon, and your attitude toward risk.

Returns-based Style Analysis

Asset allocation is a very important component of a financial strategy. Comparing current investment holdings to those that match a specific risk tolerance helps identify investment strategy imbalances. By identifying these imbalances, corrections can be implemented to achieve the desired overall performance.

In order to compare current allocations among asset classes to recommended allocations, the current investments must be analyzed and broken down to the asset class components. As mutual funds may invest in a number of different securities across a wide range of asset classes, it is particularly important to analyze the holdings within these funds to evaluate exposure to different asset classes. One method of analyzing the holdings of funds is to use a statistical method called returns-based style analysis.

Developed by Nobel Laureate William Sharpe in 1990, returns-based style analysis seeks to determine what a fund's overall "style" or behavior has been over a defined historical period. This behavior is communicated in the form of a style benchmark, or mix of basic asset classes. This is done with the assumption that a historical analysis of return volatility is applicable to the prediction of future fund behavior and manager performance.

It is important to note that returns-based style analysis does not attempt to find the exact investment holdings of a mutual fund. A prospectus or shareholder report can tell you a fund's objective or current holdings, but they cannot explain the past and present behavior of the fund. A fund's stated objective does not guarantee that it will behave in that fashion. Using statistical methods, returns-based style analysis discerns the mix of benchmark asset classes that is most similar to the fund's actual behavior. It is not the actual holdings, but the behavior and economics behind the fund that are of primary importance in this forum. A fund may call itself a "growth fund" but behave like a value fund and, therefore, should be used as a value component of an asset mix.

For example, a domestic equity mutual fund investing in stocks that derive a majority of their revenue from sales abroad will clearly be influenced by factors in foreign economies. If the foreign economies go into recession, the fund will be affected. In this way, the fund, although domestic, responds to factors in foreign economies with a manner similar to an international equity fund. This is essential information in mapping the fund into as asset mix derived from basic asset classes.

Asset Allocation Questionnaire

Different investors have different risk tolerances. Much of the difference stems from time horizon. That is, someone with a short investment time horizon is less able to withstand losses. The remainder of the difference is attributable to the individual's appetite for risk. Volatility can be nerve-wracking for many people and they are more comfortable when they can avoid it. However, there is a definite relationship between risk and return. Investors need to recognize this risk/return trade-off. The following risk tolerance questionnaire has been designed to measure an individual's ability (time horizon) and willingness (risk tolerance) to accept uncertainties in their investment's performance. The total score recommends which of the five risk profiles is most appropriate for the investor.

Time Horizon

1. When do you expect to begin withdrawing money from your investment account?

    a.   Less than 1 year
    b.   1 to 2 years
    c.   3 to 4 years
    d.   5 to 7 years
    e.   8 to 10 years
    f.   11 years or more

2. Once you begin withdrawing money from your investment account, how long do you expect the withdrawals to last?

    a.   I plan to take a lump sum distribution
    b.   1 to 4 years
    c.   5 to 7 years
    d.   8 to 10 years
    e.   11 years or more

Continued...

Risk Tolerance

3. Inflation, the rise in prices over time, can erode your investment return. Long-term investors should be aware that, if portfolio returns are less than the inflation rate, their ability to purchase goods and services in the future might actually **decline**. However, portfolios with long-term returns that significantly exceed inflation are associated with a higher degree of risk.

    Which of the following portfolios is most consistent with your investment philosophy?

    a.   **Portfolio 1** will most likely exceed long-term inflation by a significant margin and has a high degree of risk.
    b.   **Portfolio 2** will most likely exceed long-term inflation by a moderate margin and has a high to moderate degree of risk.
    c.   **Portfolio 3** will most likely exceed long-term inflation by a small margin and has a moderate degree of risk.
    d.   **Portfolio 4** will most likely match long-term inflation and has a low degree of risk.

4. Portfolios with the highest average returns also tend to have the highest chance of short-term losses. The table below provides the average dollar return of four hypothetical investments of $100,000 and the possibility of losing money (ending value of less than $100,000) over a **one-year holding period**. Please select the portfolio with which you are most comfortable.

    Probabilities After 1 Year

	Possible Average Value at the End of One Year	Chance of Losing Money at the End of One Year
a. Portfolio A	$105,000	24%
b. Portfolio B	$107,000	27%
c. Portfolio C	$108,000	29%
d. Portfolio D	$110,000	31%

5. Investing involves a trade-off between risk and return. Historically, investors who have received high long-term average returns have experienced greater fluctuations in the value of their portfolio and more frequent short-term losses than investors in more conservative investments have. Considering the above, which statement best describes your investment goals?

    a.   **Protect the value of my account.** In order to minimize the chance for loss, I am willing to accept the lower long-term returns provided by conservative investments.
    b.   **Keep risk to a minimum** while trying to achieve slightly higher returns than the returns provided by investments that are more conservative.
    c.   **Balance** moderate levels of risk with moderate levels of returns.
    d.   **Maximize long-term investment returns.** I am willing to accept large and sometimes dramatic fluctuations in the value of my investments.

Continued...

6. Historically, markets have experienced downturns, both short-term and prolonged, followed by market recoveries. Suppose you owned a well-diversified portfolio that fell by 20% (i.e. $1,000 initial investment would now be worth $800) over a short period, consistent with the overall market. Assuming you still have 10 years until you begin withdrawals, how would you react?

    a. I would **not** change my portfolio.
    b. I would **wait at least one year** before changing to options that are more conservative.
    c. I would **wait at least three months** before changing to options that are more conservative.
    d. I would **immediately** change to options that are more conservative.

7. The following graph shows the hypothetical results of four sample portfolios over a one-year holding period. The best potential and worst potential gains and losses are presented. Note that the portfolio with the best potential gain also has the largest potential loss.

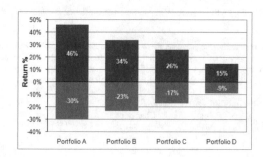

    Which of these portfolios would you prefer to hold?

    a. Portfolio A
    b. Portfolio B
    c. Portfolio C
    d. Portfolio D

8. I am comfortable with investments that may frequently experience large declines in value if there is a potential for higher returns.

    a. Agree
    b. Disagree
    c. Strongly disagree

_____   _____

Client Signature   Date

Importance of Strategic Asset Allocation
Contributing Factors of Portfolio Performance

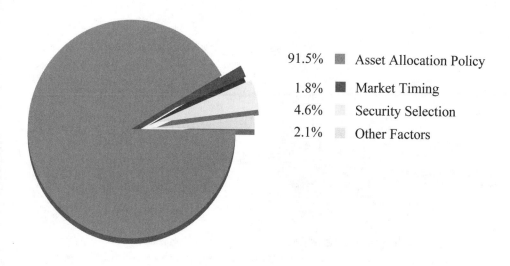

91.5% ▪ Asset Allocation Policy

1.8% ▪ Market Timing

4.6% ▪ Security Selection

2.1% ▪ Other Factors

Gary Brinson, Brian Singer and Gilbert Beebower presented a framework for determining the contributions of various aspects of the investment management process: asset allocation policy, active asset allocation, and security selection to the total return of investment portfolios. After comparing the returns from 82 major pension plans, during the years 1977 to 1987, they concluded that 91.5% of the portfolio performance is attributed to asset allocation. Market timing (buying and selling an investment at the most favorable time) and selection of individual securities can account for less than 10% of the portfolio's performance.

Source: Brinson, Singer and Beebower. "Determinants of Performance II: An Update," *Financial Analysts Journal*, May-June 1991, pp 40-48.

Power of Compounding
Hypothetical Investment in Stocks

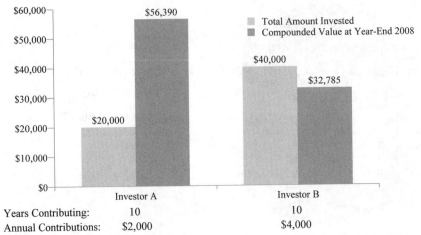

	Investor A	Investor B
Years Contributing:	10	10
Annual Contributions:	$2,000	$4,000

Past performance is no guarantee of future results. This is for illustrative purposes only and not indicative of any investment. An investment cannot be made directly in an index.
© 2009 Ibbotson Associates, Inc., a wholly owned subsidiary of Morningstar, Inc. All rights reserved. EISI has engaged Ibbotson to develop proprietary asset allocation tools for educational purposes. Ibbotson has granted to EISI a license for use thereof.

Power of Compounding
It's easy to procrastinate when it comes to initiating a long-term investment plan. However, the sooner you begin, the more likely it is that the plan will succeed.

This image illustrates the effects of compounding over time. Investor A began investing in stocks at the beginning of 1989, investing $2,000 each year for 10 years. After 10 years, Investor A stopped contributing to the portfolio but allowed it to grow for the next 10 years. The $20,000 outlay grew to $56,390 by year-end 2008.

Investor B postponed investing for 10 years. At the beginning of 1999, Investor B began investing $4,000 each year in stocks for 10 years. The $40,000 outlay of Investor B actually declined to $32,782 by year-end 2008.

By starting early, and thereby taking advantage of compounding, Investor A accumulated $23,605 more than Investor B, while still investing $20,000 less.

Returns and principal invested in stocks are not guaranteed. The data assumes reinvestment of income and does not account for taxes or transaction costs.

About the data
Stocks are represented by the Standard & Poor's 500®, which is an unmanaged group of securities and considered to be representative of the stock market in general. An investment cannot be made directly in an index.

Presented by: The Abundant Life Institute

Financial Needs in the Event of John's Disability

Disability is something most people don't like to think about. But the chances of your becoming disabled are probably greater than you realize. Studies show that a 20-year-old worker has a 3-in-10 chance of becoming disabled before reaching retirement age.[1] In fact, the Census Bureau reports there are currently over twenty-one million people of working age who are disabled.[2]

This disability needs analysis shows the impact a disability can have on your financial situation.

Your current annual income is $87,500 and your current long-term disability coverage provides $0 per year. Your disability goal is to provide 60% of your current income, or $52,500.

Without additional coverage you may need to deplete your savings and investments to meet your ongoing living expenses.

About Disability Income Insurance...

When purchasing disability income protection, there are a number of options to consider:

- Protection against inflation for future Benefits paid, referred to as Cost of Living Adjustment (COLA).

- Non-cancelable, guaranteed renewable provisions.

- Various waiting periods are available. The longer the waiting period, the lower the premium.

- Policies offer varying benefit periods. The longer the period covered by the policy, the higher the premium.

- Some Policies provide "Own Occupation" coverage and will pay benefits if the insured is unable to work in their specialized field.

Disability Income

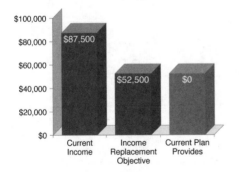

A word about Social Security[1]...

It's important that you understand how Social Security defines "disability." That's because other programs have different definitions for disability. Some programs pay for partial disability or for short-term disability. Social Security does **not.**

The Social Security Administration uses the strict definition of disability. Disability under Social Security is based on your inability to work. You will be considered disabled if you cannot do work you did before, and the SSA decides that you cannot adjust to other work because of your medical condition. Your disability also must last or be expected to last for at least a year or to result in death.

For these reasons, this analysis does not include any potential benefits from Social Security.

[1] Source: SSA Publication No. 05-10029, November 2008.
[2] Source: U.S. Census Bureau, Disability Status 2000, Employment disability age 16-64.

Disability Needs Analysis Detail
In the event of John's Disability

In the first year following a disability

After	Salary to Replace	Desired Replacement	Existing Insurance	(Shortage)/ Surplus
1 Month	$87,500	$52,500	$0	($52,500)
2 Months	$87,500	$52,500	$0	($52,500)
3 Months	$87,500	$52,500	$0	($52,500)
6 Months	$87,500	$52,500	$0	($52,500)

In the years following a disability

	John's Age	Salary to Replace	Desired Replacement	Existing Insurance	(Shortage)/ Surplus
1 Year	42	$91,000	$54,600	$0	($54,600)
2 Years	43	$94,640	$56,784	$0	($56,784)
5 Years	46	$106,457	$63,874	$0	($63,874)
10 Years	51	$129,521	$77,713	$0	($77,713)
Age 64		$215,663	$129,398	$0	($129,398)
Age 65		$224,289	$134,573	$0	($134,573)

Disability Policies

Policy Name	Monthly Benefit	Type	Waiting Period	Benefit Period	COLA
No policies are listed.					

Assumptions

Income Replacement % of John's Income	60%
Inflation	4.00%

Presented by: The Abundant Life Institute

Financial Needs in the Event of Jane's Disability

Disability is something most people don't like to think about. But the chances of your becoming disabled are probably greater than you realize. Studies show that a 20-year-old worker has a 3-in-10 chance of becoming disabled before reaching retirement age.[1] In fact, the Census Bureau reports there are currently over twenty-one million people of working age who are disabled.[2]

This disability needs analysis shows the impact a disability can have on your financial situation.

Your current annual income is $42,500 and your current long-term disability coverage provides $0 per year. Your disability goal is to provide 60% of your current income, or $25,500.

Without additional coverage you may need to deplete your savings and investments to meet your ongoing living expenses.

About Disability Income Insurance...

When purchasing disability income protection, there are a number of options to consider:

• Protection against inflation for future Benefits paid, referred to as Cost of Living Adjustment (COLA).

• Non-cancelable, guaranteed renewable provisions.

• Various waiting periods are available. The longer the waiting period, the lower the premium.

• Policies offer varying benefit periods. The longer the period covered by the policy, the higher the premium.

• Some Policies provide "Own Occupation" coverage and will pay benefits if the insured is unable to work in their specialized field.

Disability Income

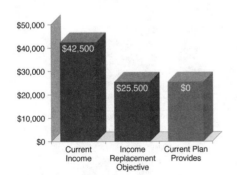

[1]Source: SSA Publication No. 05-10029, November 2008.
[2]Source: U.S. Census Bureau, Disability Status 2000, Employment disability age 16-64.

A word about Social Security[1]...

It's important that you understand how Social Security defines "disability." That's because other programs have different definitions for disability. Some programs pay for partial disability or for short-term disability. Social Security does **not.**

The Social Security Administration uses the strict definition of disability. Disability under Social Security is based on your inability to work. You will be considered disabled if you cannot do work you did before, and the SSA decides that you cannot adjust to other work because of your medical condition. Your disability also must last or be expected to last for at least a year or to result in death.

For these reasons, this analysis does not include any potential benefits from Social Security.

Presented by: The Abundant Life Institute

Disability Needs Analysis Detail
In the event of Jane's Disability

In the first year following a disability

After	Salary to Replace	Desired Replacement	Existing Insurance	(Shortage)/ Surplus
1 Month	$42,500	$25,500	$7,200	($18,300)
2 Months	$42,500	$25,500	$7,200	($18,300)
3 Months	$42,500	$25,500	$7,200	($18,300)
6 Months	$42,500	$25,500	$0	($25,500)

In the years following a disability

	Jane's Age	Salary to Replace	Desired Replacement	Existing Insurance	(Shortage)/ Surplus
1 Year	39	$44,200	$26,520	$0	($26,520)
2 Years	40	$45,968	$27,581	$0	($27,581)
5 Years	43	$51,708	$31,025	$0	($31,025)
10 Years	48	$62,910	$37,746	$0	($37,746)
Age 64		$117,830	$70,698	$0	($70,698)
Age 65		$122,543	$73,526	$0	($73,526)

Disability Policies

Policy Name	Monthly Benefit	Type	Waiting Period	Benefit Period	COLA
	$600	Group	1 month	3 months	4.00%

Assumptions

Income Replacement % of Jane's Income	60%
Inflation	4.00%

Disability Income Insurance

Most people have insurance coverage on their homes, autos, etc., but many have not realized the value of their future earnings may far exceed the value of their tangible assets. If their future earnings cease because of an accident or illness, the loss of income could present serious financial problems.

Disability income insurance policies can help replace a portion of the loss of income due to disability during one's working years. The following is a list of features disability income policies can include:

- Non-cancelable, guaranteed renewable provisions.
- Protection against inflation for future benefits paid, referred to as Cost of Living Adjustment (COLA).
- Various elimination periods before benefits begin, typically 30, 60, or 90 days, 6 months, or one year. The longer the elimination period, the lower the premium. A person's liquid reserves, income, and existing disability income insurance must be considered when selecting an appropriate elimination period.
- Some policies provide "Own Occupation" coverage and will pay benefits if those insured are unable to work in their specialized field.
- Policies offer varying benefit periods. Some policies, for example, offer a lifetime benefit if the disability was caused by an accident, and to age 65 for a disability caused by illness. Disability can last for a long time. The longer the period covered by the policy, the higher the premium.
- Disability policies may be purchased by an individual or by a company. Others may be acquired on a group or association basis.

Other types of Disability Income Insurance policies include:

- Key Employee Disability Insurance - When the employer owns the policy, the insurance benefits can provide funds to help cover expenses related to the loss of services of a disabled employee, such as hiring and training a replacement.
- Disability Buy-out - Funds can be provided to help effect a buy-out of a disabled business owner or professional under the terms of a Buy-Sell agreement.
- Business Overhead Expense - If a business owner or professional becomes disabled, these policies can provide funds to help cover ongoing expenses such as rent, employee salaries, etc., to keep the business open during the period of disability.

Of Special Note: Some policies pay benefits when earnings drop by a certain percentage due to a disability. Others require a physician's certification to pay or continue benefits. Also, some policies provide for partial or residual disability benefits where the insured can perform some, but not all of their duties. Policy language and provisions should be carefully reviewed.

Disability - Sources of Income

Savings

If you save 10% annually, one
year of disability could wipe out
10 years of savings.

Family, Friends and Charity

Do you want to depend on
them?

Other Household Income

Is it enough to cover all of your
expenses?

Sell Investments

Will you get a fair price?

Loan

Without an income, will anyone
lend you money?

Social Security

Will you qualify?*

When disability occurs, most options, except insured income replacement, may be inadequate or quickly exhausted.

Disability is difficult enough - disability without income is even worse. Disability income insurance is a sound long-term solution to a long-term disability.

*You may be eligible for Social Security benefits after you have been disabled for five months and if the disability is expected to last 12 months or result in death.

Presented by: The Abundant Life Institute

Odds of Death and Disability

Odds of Death At Age	Within 15 Years	Within 30 Years	Before Age 65
25	1 in 55	1 in 15	1 in 6
30	1 in 44	1 in 10	1 in 6
35	1 in 30	1 in 7	1 in 7
40	1 in 20	1 in 4	1 in 7
45	1 in 13	1 in 3	1 in 7
50	1 in 8	1 in 2	1 in 8

Odds of Disability At Age	Within 15 Years	Within 30 Years	Before Age 65
25	1 in 40	1 in 11	1 in 5
30	1 in 33	1 in 8	1 in 5
35	1 in 24	1 in 5	1 in 5
40	1 in 15	1 in 4	1 in 5
45	1 in 10	1 in 3	1 in 6
50	1 in 6	1 in 2	1 in 6

> Proper planning for death and disability should be considered by everyone.

Source for odds of death: 2001 Commissioners Standard Ordinary Table for Male, Age Last Birthday.
Source for odds of disability: 1985 Commissioners Individual Disability Table for Male, Occupation Class 1, 90-day elimination.

Financial Needs in the Event of John's Death

This survivor needs analysis shows the impact John's death can have on your family. Funds need to be available for both Cash Needs and a family's continuing Income Needs. John and Jane, you need $380,000 for your immediate cash needs. Cash Needs include:

• A Final Expenses fund for medical, legal, funeral, and other expenses

• A Debt Payment Fund to pay off your debts, including your mortgage

• An Emergency Reserve Fund for unexpected bills not readily payable from current income

Total Immediate Cash Needs: $380,000

■ Final Expenses Fund	$10,000
■ Debt Payment Fund	$337,500
■ Emergency Fund	$32,500

After a death, income generally comes from four different sources:

• Social Security
• Savings and Investments
• Life Insurance Proceeds
• Survivor's Earnings

This survivor needs analysis assumes that 70% of total household income be available after the death of a wage earner while there are children at home and 50% thereafter.

Based on the above assumptions, this survivor needs analysis suggests that you may not meet your goals. Your current household income is $130,000. If John were to die today, it is estimated that your assets would be sufficient to meet your family's Immediate Cash Needs. However, your family's Income Needs will only be 57% satisfied. To provide for your family's needs in the event of death you will need approximately $1,299,666 of additional capital.

Total Income Needs: $1,477,534

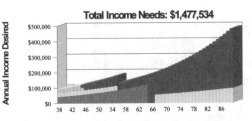

Jane's Age

■ Deficit ■ Capital Withdrawals ■ Social Security ■ Other Income

Summary	
Cash Needs:	$380,000
Income Needs:	1,477,534
Less Present Funds	*557,868*
Additional Capital Needs	**$1,299,666**

Survivor Needs Analysis Detail
In the Event of John's Death

Assumptions

Income Replacement % of Total Household Income with Dependents	70%
Income Replacement % of Total Household Income without Dependents	50%
Inflation	4.00%
Survivor Rate of Return	5.00%
Jane's Mortality	90

Income Objective

Jane's Age	Income Need %	Annual Need (Today's Dollars)	Annual Need (Future Dollars)	Capital Value
38	70%	$91,000	$91,000	$1,478,612
56	50%	65,000	131,678	1,560,468

Total Capital Needed to Provide Income Objective	**$3,039,081**

Income Sources

Jane's Income Sources	Payment In Today's Dollars	From	To	COLA	First Year's Payment	Capital Value
Employment	$42,500	38	65	4.00%	$42,500	$993,715
Social Security	25,574	38	90	2.50%	25,574	567,831

Total Income Sources	**$1,561,546**

Capital Needed to Meet Income Goals	**$1,477,534**

Immediate Cash Needs

Final Expenses		$10,000
Debt Payment Fund		$337,500
Mortgage	110,000	
Condo	218,000	
Car	9,500	
Emergency Reserve Fund		$32,500

Total Immediate Cash Needs	**$380,000**

Total Capital Needed to Meet Objectives	**$1,857,534**

Continued...

Capital Available Account Name/ Asset Name	Market Value
CD	$23,000
I Bond	3,000
Money Market 2	27,224
Money Market	13,668
Money Market 3	10,000
Blended Acct	32,134
Current 401K	7,871
Old 401K	34,971
401K	25,000
IRA	21,000
Life Insurance	360,000
Total Capital Available	**$557,868**

Additional Capital Needed to Meet Objectives	**$1,299,666**

Presented by: The Abundant Life Institute

Survivor Needs Analysis Timeline in the Event of John's Death

		Beginning Balance:			$177,868
Jane's Age	Annual Income Desired	Social Security	Other Income	Interest And Dividends	Balance
38	$91,000	$25,574	$42,500	$8,277	$163,219
39	94,640	25,894	44,200	7,501	146,174
40	98,426	26,210	45,968	6,603	126,530
41	102,363	26,521	47,807	5,573	104,068
42	106,457	26,825	49,719	4,399	78,554
43	110,715	27,123	51,708	3,071	49,740
44	115,144	27,413	53,776	1,574	17,359
45	119,750	27,695	55,927	(103)	(18,871)
46	124,540	27,968	58,164	(1,976)	(59,255)
47	129,521	28,231	60,491	(4,059)	(104,114)
48	134,702	28,483	62,910	(6,370)	(153,793)
49	140,090	28,723	65,427	(8,925)	(208,657)
50	145,694	28,951	68,044	(11,742)	(269,098)
51	151,522	29,164	70,766	(14,842)	(335,532)
52	157,583	29,363	73,596	(18,245)	(408,401)
53	163,886	29,545	76,540	(21,974)	(488,176)
54	170,441	29,500	79,602	(26,058)	(575,573)
55	177,259	30,237	82,786	(30,505)	(670,314)
56	131,678	0	86,097	(34,741)	(750,636)
57	136,945	0	89,541	(38,806)	(836,846)
58	142,423	0	93,123	(43,168)	(929,314)
59	148,120	0	96,848	(47,844)	(1,028,430)
60	154,045	0	100,722	(52,855)	(1,134,608)
61	160,207	0	104,750	(58,221)	(1,248,286)
62	166,615	0	108,940	(63,965)	(1,369,925)
63	173,279	0	113,298	(70,109)	(1,500,014)
64	180,211	0	117,830	(76,678)	(1,639,073)
65	187,419	0	0	(86,992)	(1,913,483)
66	194,916	0	0	(100,914)	(2,209,313)
67	202,712	55,623	0	(114,420)	(2,470,822)
68	210,821	57,014	0	(127,676)	(2,752,305)
69	219,254	58,439	0	(141,938)	(3,055,058)
70	228,024	59,900	0	(157,272)	(3,380,454)
71	237,145	61,397	0	(173,747)	(3,729,949)
72	246,631	62,932	0	(191,436)	(4,105,082)
73	256,496	64,506	0	(210,415)	(4,507,488)
74	266,756	66,118	0	(230,768)	(4,938,893)
75	277,426	67,771	0	(252,580)	(5,401,128)
76	288,523	69,465	0	(275,945)	(5,896,130)

Continued...

77	300,064	71,202	0	(300,959)	(6,425,951)
78	312,066	72,982	0	(327,724)	(6,992,760)
79	324,549	74,807	0	(356,351)	(7,598,853)
80	337,531	76,677	0	(386,955)	(8,246,662)
81	351,032	78,594	0	(419,657)	(8,938,757)
82	365,073	80,559	0	(454,586)	(9,677,858)
83	379,676	82,573	0	(491,879)	(10,466,841)
84	394,863	84,637	0	(531,681)	(11,308,749)
85	410,658	86,753	0	(574,145)	(12,206,799)
86	427,084	88,922	0	(619,430)	(13,164,392)
87	444,168	91,145	0	(667,709)	(14,185,125)
88	461,934	93,423	0	(719,162)	(15,272,798)
89	480,412	95,759	0	(773,980)	(16,431,431)

Presented by: The Abundant Life Institute

Financial Needs in the Event of Jane's Death

This survivor needs analysis shows the impact Jane's death can have on your family. Funds need to be available for both Cash Needs and a family's continuing Income Needs. John and Jane, you need $380,000 for your immediate cash needs. Cash Needs include:

• A Final Expenses fund for medical, legal, funeral, and other expenses

• A Debt Payment Fund to pay off your debts, including your mortgage

• An Emergency Reserve Fund for unexpected bills not readily payable from current income

Total Immediate Cash Needs: $380,000

■ Final Expenses Fund	$10,000
Debt Payment Fund	$337,500
■ Emergency Fund	$32,500

After a death, income generally comes from four different sources:

• Social Security
• Savings and Investments
• Life Insurance Proceeds
• Survivor's Earnings

This survivor needs analysis assumes that 70% of total household income be available after the death of a wage earner while there are children at home and 50% thereafter.

Based on the above assumptions, this survivor needs analysis suggests that you may not meet all of your goals. Your current household income is $130,000. If Jane were to die today, it is estimated that your assets would be insufficient to meet your family's Immediate Cash Needs. Additionally, your family's Income Needs will only be 87% satisfied. To provide for your family's needs in the event of death you will need approximately $551,586 of additional capital.

Total Income Needs: $379,454

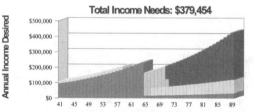

John's Age

■ Deficit   Capital Withdrawals   Social Security   ■ Other Income

Summary	
Cash Needs:	$380,000
Income Needs:	379,454
Less Present Funds	*207,868*
Additional Capital Needs	**$551,586**

Survivor Needs Analysis Detail
In the Event of Jane's Death

Assumptions	
Income Replacement % of Total Household Income with Dependents	70%
Income Replacement % of Total Household Income without Dependents	50%
Inflation	4.00%
Survivor Rate of Return	5.00%
John's Mortality	90

Income Objective

John's Age	Income Need %	Annual Need (Today's Dollars)	Annual Need (Future Dollars)	Capital Value
41	70%	$91,000	$91,000	$1,478,612
59	50%	65,000	131,678	1,442,278

Total Capital Needed to Provide Income Objective	**$2,920,891**

Income Sources

John's Income Sources	Payment In Today's Dollars	From	To	COLA	First Year's Payment	Capital Value
Employment	$87,500	41	65	4.00%	$87,500	$1,843,780
Social Security	13,349	41	90	2.50%	13,349	446,855
Condo	8,004	41	90	3.00%	8,004	250,801

Total Income Sources	**$2,541,437**

Capital Needed to Meet Income Goals	**$379,454**

Immediate Cash Needs

Final Expenses		$10,000
Debt Payment Fund		$337,500
Mortgage	110,000	
Condo	218,000	
Car	9,500	
Emergency Reserve Fund		$32,500

Total Immediate Cash Needs	**$380,000**

Total Capital Needed to Meet Objectives	**$759,454**

Continued...

Presented by: The Abundant Life Institute

Capital Available Account Name/ Asset Name	Market Value
CD	$23,000
I Bond	3,000
Money Market 2	27,224
Money Market	13,668
Money Market 3	10,000
Blended Acct	32,134
Current 401K	7,871
Old 401K	34,971
401K	25,000
IRA	21,000
Life Insurance	10,000
Total Capital Available	**$207,868**

Additional Capital Needed to Meet Objectives	**$551,586**

Survivor Needs Analysis Timeline in the Event of Jane's Death

				Beginning Balance:	($172,132)
John's Age	Annual Income Desired	Social Security	Other Income	Interest And Dividends	Balance
41	$91,000	$13,349	$95,504	($8,127)	($162,405)
42	94,640	13,683	99,244	(7,629)	(151,747)
43	98,426	14,025	103,131	(7,084)	(140,100)
44	102,363	14,376	107,172	(6,489)	(127,404)
45	106,457	14,735	111,371	(5,842)	(113,597)
46	110,715	15,104	115,736	(5,139)	(98,612)
47	115,144	15,481	120,273	(4,377)	(82,379)
48	119,750	15,868	124,988	(3,552)	(64,824)
49	124,540	16,265	129,889	(2,660)	(45,870)
50	129,521	16,671	134,983	(1,699)	(25,435)
51	134,702	17,088	140,278	(663)	(3,434)
52	140,090	17,515	145,782	452	20,225
53	145,694	17,953	151,502	1,650	45,637
54	151,522	18,402	157,448	2,936	72,901
55	157,583	18,862	163,628	4,315	102,124
56	163,886	19,334	170,053	5,792	133,416
57	170,441	19,817	176,730	7,373	166,894
58	177,259	20,313	183,671	9,063	202,681
59	131,678	0	190,885	11,726	273,614
60	136,945	0	198,384	15,332	350,386
61	142,423	0	206,179	19,233	433,375
62	148,120	0	214,282	23,447	522,985
63	154,045	0	222,704	27,995	619,639
64	160,207	0	231,459	32,897	723,789
65	166,615	0	16,270	32,148	605,593
66	173,279	0	16,759	26,072	475,144
67	180,211	51,651	17,261	20,765	384,612
68	187,419	52,943	17,779	16,094	284,008
69	194,916	54,266	18,313	10,912	172,583
70	202,712	55,623	18,862	5,182	49,538
71	210,821	57,014	19,428	(1,135)	(85,977)
72	219,254	58,439	20,011	(8,084)	(234,865)
73	228,024	59,900	20,611	(15,709)	(398,086)
74	237,145	61,397	21,229	(24,058)	(576,663)
75	246,631	62,932	21,866	(33,183)	(771,678)
76	256,496	64,506	22,522	(43,139)	(984,286)
77	266,756	66,118	23,198	(53,984)	(1,215,709)
78	277,426	67,771	23,894	(65,779)	(1,467,249)
79	288,523	69,465	24,611	(78,589)	(1,740,286)

Continued...

Presented by: The Abundant Life Institute

80	300,064	71,202	25,349	(92,485)	(2,036,283)
81	312,066	72,982	26,109	(107,539)	(2,356,798)
82	324,549	74,807	26,893	(123,830)	(2,703,478)
83	337,531	76,677	27,699	(141,441)	(3,078,074)
84	351,032	78,594	28,530	(160,460)	(3,482,442)
85	365,073	80,559	29,386	(180,980)	(3,918,551)
86	379,676	82,573	30,268	(203,100)	(4,388,487)
87	394,863	84,637	31,176	(226,926)	(4,894,464)
88	410,658	86,753	32,111	(252,567)	(5,438,825)
89	427,084	88,922	33,075	(280,142)	(6,024,055)

Types of Life Insurance

Decreasing Term
Level premiums and decreasing death benefit. No cash accumulation. Frequently used for short-term decreasing financial liabilities, like a mortgage.

Annual Renewable Term
Increasing premiums with level death benefit. No cash accumulation. The strength of term is its low cost for large death benefits, particularly beneficial to younger families with limited resources and the need for maximum protection.

Level Term
Premiums stay level for stated term. Usually 5, 10, 15, or 20 years. Level death benefit. No cash value. Frequently used to cover short or intermediate-term obligations.

Cash Value - Ordinary Life or Whole Life
Premiums and death benefit are level. Cash accumulation. Provides for long-term needs, such as survivor income for a spouse or minor children. Other uses could include paying off debt and paying estate taxes.

Universal Life
Premiums and death benefit are flexible. The monthly cost of insurance and administrative charges are deducted, the balance of the premium goes to cash values. The benefits and uses are very similar to Whole Life. Cash values can increase based on current interest rates.

Variable Life
Premiums and death benefit may be flexible. Cash accumulation is directly affected by the performance of the separate accounts selected. Clients allocate their cash values among various types of investment options such as stock funds, bond funds, money market funds, etc. Cash values may increase or decrease depending on account performance.

Single Premium Life
A single premium paid up front. Level minimum death benefit. Cash accumulation. Provides long-term security. Different tax rules generally apply.

First To Die
May have flexible premiums and death benefits. Provides death benefits at the death of the first of two or more parties covered by the policy. Most often used in business insurance situations.

Survivorship Life
May have flexible premium with a level minimum death benefit. Most often used to pay death taxes and expenses due at second death.

Mutual funds and Variable Products are sold through registered representatives only and must be accompanied by a prospectus. Read the prospectus carefully prior to investing or sending money.

Presented by: The Abundant Life Institute

Life Insurance

There are a number of types of policies, each with a different approach to fulfilling one's needs for life insurance. Key considerations are the duration of the need, premium budget, and the purpose for the need. You will also want to take into consideration your own attitude about buying policies with underlying guarantees versus policies which shift more risk to the policy owner, and issues surrounding finding the best "short-term price" versus considerations of lowest "long-term cost." Your age and your general health may also affect your policy choices.

Policy Type	Duration of need	Premium Budget	Purpose	Dominant Benefit
Term	5-15 years	Low	Short-term protection	Initially inexpensive
Whole Life	15+ years	High	Long-term protection	Guaranteed premiums
Blended Whole Life	15+ years	Medium	Long-term protection	Initially flexible premiums
Universal Life	10+ years	Medium	Long-term protection	Flexible premiums
Variable Life	20+ years	Med-High	Long-term protection	For those with tolerance for risk: an opportunity to direct the investment of policy cash values

Tax advantages, liquidity at death, family benefits … these are a few of the attributes of life insurance. And, life insurance is a product that can provide a known sum at an unknown time.

Life Expectancy Table
Life Expectancy in Years

At Age	Male	Female	At Age	Male	Female	At Age	Male	Female
0	74.83	79.96	30	46.58	51.05	60	20.36	23.53
1	74.40	79.45	31	45.64	50.08	61	19.60	22.71
2	73.43	78.49	32	44.70	49.11	62	18.85	21.89
3	72.46	77.51	33	43.76	48.14	63	18.11	21.08
4	71.47	76.52	34	42.83	47.18	64	17.38	20.29
5	70.49	75.54	35	41.89	46.22	65	16.67	19.50
6	69.50	74.55	36	40.96	45.26	66	15.96	18.72
7	68.52	73.56	37	40.04	44.30	67	15.27	17.95
8	67.53	72.57	38	39.11	43.35	68	14.59	17.19
9	66.54	71.58	39	38.19	42.40	69	13.93	16.45
10	65.55	70.58	40	37.28	41.46	70	13.27	15.72
11	64.55	69.59	41	36.36	40.52	71	12.64	15.01
12	63.56	68.60	42	35.46	39.58	72	12.01	14.31
13	62.57	67.61	43	34.56	38.65	73	11.41	13.62
14	61.59	66.62	44	33.67	37.72	74	10.81	12.95
15	60.61	65.64	45	32.78	36.80	75	10.24	12.29
16	59.65	64.66	46	31.90	35.88	76	9.68	11.64
17	58.70	63.68	47	31.03	34.96	77	9.14	11.01
18	57.75	62.71	48	30.17	34.06	78	8.62	10.40
19	56.81	61.74	49	29.31	33.15	79	8.11	9.80
20	55.88	60.76	50	28.46	32.25	80	7.62	9.22
21	54.95	59.79	51	27.62	31.35	81	7.15	8.65
22	54.02	58.82	52	26.79	30.46	82	6.70	8.11
23	53.10	57.84	53	25.96	29.57	83	6.26	7.59
24	52.17	56.87	54	25.14	28.68	84	5.84	7.09
25	51.25	55.90	55	24.33	27.81	85	5.45	6.62
26	50.32	54.93	56	23.52	26.94	86	5.08	6.17
27	49.38	53.96	57	22.71	26.07	87	4.73	5.74
28	48.45	52.99	58	21.92	25.22	88	4.40	5.33
29	47.52	52.02	59	21.13	24.37	89	4.09	4.96

Source: Social Security Administration, Period Life Table, 2004, updated March 2008.

Presented by: The Abundant Life Institute

College Needs Analysis

Will you have enough money when it is time to send your children to college? The earlier you begin setting money aside for college, the more likely you are to achieve your goals.

You currently have $0 set aside and you are saving $0 a month at 5.00% for college expenses.

This college analysis suggests that you will meet your goal.

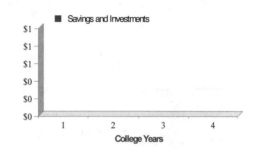

Projected College Costs

Sarah	$0
Total	**$0**

Total College Cost in Today's Dollars

Sarah

Monthly savings alternative

Begin saving an additional $0 per month for the next 0 years. Savings goals under $0.50 round to zero.

Why should you begin preparing for college needs now?

If you wait until it's time for college to begin, you lose the advantage of spreading the costs over many years.

If you have to borrow money to pay for college, the amount of the loan and interest will have to be repaid.

If you start now, the interest earned on your savings will reduce the total amount that you need to save.

College Needs Analysis Detail

Goal Summary

Name/ School	Age	Annual Need (today's Dollars)	Years Until Needed	Number Years Needed	Present Value of Total Cost	Percentage To Be Funded	Present Value of Total Cost To Be Funded
Sarah	0	$0	18	4	$0	100%	$0

Present Value of Total Need   **$0**

Savings Summary

Current Savings	$0
Monthly Savings	
$0 per month for 21 years at 5.00% grows to $0	
In today's dollars that is:	$0

Present Value of Savings   **$0**

Single Sum Needed Today to Fund Shortage   **$0**

Additional Monthly Savings Required

Starting Age	Amount Needed
John's age 41 for 0 years	**$0**

Assumptions

College Cost Inflation Rate	6.00%
Average Rate of Return	5.00%

This analysis assumes that savings will continue until the start of the last year of college.

College Funding Techniques

Qualified State Tuition Programs (Section 529 Plans) - Section 529 Plans are authorized under Internal Revenue Code Section 529 and are sponsored by the individual states. These programs allow parents, grandparents and non-relatives to contribute money to an account of which the child is the beneficiary. There are two types of plans: a prepaid tuition plan and a savings plan. Prepaid tuition plans guarantee that the investment will at least keep pace with increases in college tuition. Restrictions may apply regarding who may contribute to the prepaid plan and which schools are eligible. Savings plans are managed investment funds that can be more flexible. Income inside these plans is not currently taxable. Funds withdrawn to pay for qualified education expenses are also free from federal income tax. Other, nonqualified withdrawals are subject to ordinary income tax and may be subject to an additional 10% penalty tax. The child may attend almost any accredited college, university, or trade school regardless of location. These plans, having no income restrictions, are available to almost anyone. Unlike UGMAs and UTMAs (discussed below), the donor retains control over the funds. Tax-free rollovers from one plan to another are allowed for the benefit of the same beneficiary once per year. Because contributions are considered completed gifts, the plans may offer estate planning advantages. Some plans offer preferential state tax treatment. Funds may be transferred, if necessary, to certain family members of the beneficiary without penalty. Taxable withdrawals may avoid the additional 10% penalty tax if they occur on account of death, disability or receipt of a scholarship.

The availability of the tax or other benefits mentioned above may be conditioned on meeting certain requirements.

Investors should consider the investment objectives, risks, charges and expenses associated with 529 plans carefully before investing. More information about 529 plans is available in the issuer's official statement, which should be read carefully before investing.

Coverdell Education Savings Accounts - Taxpayers may deposit up to $2,000 per year into a Coverdell Education Savings Account (ESA) for a child under age 18. Parents, grandparents, other family members, friends, and children themselves may contribute to the Coverdell ESA, provided that the total contributions during the taxable year do not exceed the $2,000 limit. Amounts deposited into the account grow tax-free until distributed, and the child will not owe tax on any withdrawal from the account if the child's qualified higher education expenses at an eligible educational institution for the year equal or exceed the amount of withdrawal. Eligible expenses also include elementary and secondary school (K-12) costs and the cost of computer equipment, internet services, and software. If the child does not need the money for post-secondary education, the account balance can be rolled over to the Coverdell ESA of certain family members who can use it for their education expenses. Amounts withdrawn from a Coverdell ESA that exceed the child's qualified education expenses in a taxable year are generally subject to income tax and to an additional tax of 10%.

Uniform Gift to Minors Act (UGMA) and Uniform Transfer to Minors Act (UTMA) - A donor may make an outright gift to a custodial account for the benefit of a minor child. The parent or custodian may retain responsibility of management of the assets in the account subject to the terms of the act. The standard rules regarding gift tax exclusions apply, including the annual $13,000 limit. The donor may choose to contribute from a number of assets, such as stocks, bonds, mutual funds or real estate. The funds may be used for any purpose, including education. One possible problem with the UGMA and UTMA is that upon reaching a certain age, specified by each state's laws, the child has full discretionary control over the accumulated assets and may choose to use such assets for purposes other than college funding.

Cash Value Life Insurance - Parents, grandparents, or other family members may gift premiums, and the cash value build-up inside the policy is tax deferred during the accumulation period. When the time for college arrives, the needed cash may be withdrawn from the policy (generally on a tax-free basis up to the amount of the premiums paid), or the cash values can be borrowed from the policy. In most cases, loans or withdrawals will reduce the policy's cash value and death benefit. If the policy is surrendered or lapses, taxes may be due. If the insured dies before the child goes to school, then the life insurance proceeds can be used to fund education expenses.

U.S. Savings Bonds Interest earned by U.S. Series EE Savings Bonds is free from state income taxes. All or some of the interest may also be free from federal income taxes if the bonds are used for qualified higher education expenses. The exclusion from federal tax is subject to an income phase-out. The bonds must be registered in the parent's name and redeemed in the same year as the eligible tuition and fees are paid.

College Costs - by Region

| | Tuition and Fees | | 10 Year Change | Percentage Change |
	1998-1999	2008-2009		
National				
Two-Year Public	$1,554	$2,402	$848	55%
Four-Year Public	3,247	6,585	3,338	103%
Four-Year Private	14,709	25,143	10,434	71%
New England				
Two-Year Public	2,302	3,698	1,396	61%
Four-Year Public	4,635	8,602	3,967	86%
Four-Year Private	19,211	31,680	12,469	65%
Middle States				
Two-Year Public	2,622	3,554	932	36%
Four-Year Public	4,201	7,565	3,364	80%
Four-Year Private	15,381	26,703	11,322	74%
South				
Two-Year Public	1,235	2,362	1,127	91%
Four-Year Public	2,675	5,412	2,737	102%
Four-Year Private	12,636	21,773	9,137	72%
Midwest				
Two-Year Public	1,834	3,065	1,231	67%
Four-Year Public	3,647	7,785	4,138	113%
Four-Year Private	14,007	23,431	9,424	67%
Southwest				
Two-Year Public	995	1,822	827	83%
Four-Year Public	2,526	6,421	3,895	154%
Four-Year Private	10,701	21,116	10,415	97%
West				
Two-Year Public	1,053	1,292	239	23%
Four-Year Public	2,660	5,428	2,768	104%
Four-Year Private	14,290	24,610	10,320	72%

Source: 2008 Trends in College Pricing © 2008 The College Board. All rights reserved.

 Presented by: The Abundant Life Institute